Books by Kevin Johnson

Early Teen Devotionals

Can I Be a Christian Without Being Weird?

Could Someone Wake Me Up Before I Drool on the Desk?

Does Anybody Know What Planet My Parents Are From?

So Who Says I Have to Act My Age?

Who Should I Listen To?

Why Can't My Life Be a Summer Vacation?

Why Is God Looking for Friends?

Books for Teens

Catch the Wave!

Look Who's Toast Now!

To find out more about Kevin Johnson's books,
visit his Web site: http://www.thewave.org

To Jeff

Snack on a White Castle Slider today
In case the world ends tomorrow

KEVIN JOHNSON pastored a group of more than 400 sixth through ninth graders at Elmbrook Church in metro Milwaukee. While his training includes an M.Div. from Fuller Theological Seminary and a B.A. in English and Print Journalism from the University of Wisconsin–River Falls, his current interests run along the lines of cycling, guitar, and shortwave radio. His eight-to-five pastime—editing books—takes place at Bethany House Publishers, where he is the senior editor for adult nonfiction. Kevin and his wife, Lyn, live in Minnesota with their three children, Nathaniel, Karin, and Elise.

CONTENTS

Some say the world will end in fire,
Some say in ice.
From what I've tasted of desire
I hold with those who favor fire.
But if it had to perish twice,
I think I know enough of hate
To say that for destruction ice
Is also great
And would suffice.

—Robert Frost (1874-1963)
United States poet
"Fire and Ice"

1

Ticking Toward Doomsday

You'd squabbled with friends at school, and when practice ran late they rudely ditched you and drove off.

Stranded.

You call home, but all you get is your own muffled voice on the answering machine.

No ride.

You don't want to walk home, much less walk alone on a dead winter night. But you don't know what else to do. You button tight and turn up your collar to keep wind from biting down your back.

Halfway home a car approaches from behind. The back part of your brain wonders why it takes forever to pass. You slow, waiting for the car to move on. The car slows more. You step. The car edges closer. You step again. Headlights toss your eerie shape down the road. Brakes grind as the car nudges toward you, and the engine growls so close you brace for the bumper to hit the back of your knees. You think about bolting. Instead you freeze.

Any bets on what's creeping up on you?

Maybe your mom got your message.

You hope it's your teammates toying with your mind, ready to be friends again and spare you a cold walk home.

There's always a chance it's Ed McMahon tooling around in the Publisher's Clearinghouse van, tracking you down to tell you you're instantly rich.

It could be aliens flying ultra low and slow—a spacepod with bad brakes.

Or it might be your worst nightmare—a predator, a bloodsucking scaryman, a charter member of ax-aholics anonymous.

It's hard to tell what lurks when you walk down the road.

It's like your future. You never know what awaits you.

Peering Into Your Future

Maybe you expect a bright future. *Shades!* You're studying hard, working two jobs, and keeping your nose out of trouble. Neat and predictable, you've made your plans—bought your ticket, chosen your destination, booked an ultimo rental car. You envision you and all your friends packed into a red Ferrari convertible, wind whipping your hair into wild 'dos.

You're in the driver's seat. Sun-kissed. *In control.*

But maybe not. Maybe your future will beat you up, duct tape your mouth, and drive you who-knows-where. You're tossed in the trunk. Locked in the dark. Totally *out of control.*

Your future is as much a walk in the unknown as a lonely stroll down a dark winter road. Ponder these:

- Maybe you'll strike it rich. In Ontario's Lotto 649, it's one chance in 13.6 million.
- You could get hit by lightning. You've got a one in 3.4 million chance in the next 365 days.
- Chance you'll freeze to death? One in 370,000. Less in

Florida. More in Minnesota.

- Truly scary one: If you're a girl, you face a one in twelve chance of being a victim of attempted or actual rape during your lifetime.
- If you're a man in Germany, there's a one in seven chance you'll change your underwear today.
- Chance that someday you'll get married in June: one in nine.
- Chance that you won't live with your father this year: two in five.
- Chance that you'll be killed by a falling vending machine: one in 130 million. This year. Heads up.
- If you're a guy, there's a one in five chance that sometime you'll spend a night in jail.
- Wondering if your dad or mom will yell at you today? Also one in five.
- Chance that a space rock will hit the earth and you'll spend the rest of your life as a hunter-gatherer: one in 10,000. In your lifetime. No joke.
- You have a one in three chance of developing nearsightedness in college. Fetch some prescription shades.
- You have a ninety-two percent likelihood of passing the Dunkin' Donuts Training Center's six-week training course.
- And there's a fifty-fifty chance you'll have a pizza delivered to your house in the next ninety days. (Way higher if you have Pizza Hut programmed on your phone's auto-dialer.)

Think about this one: What's the chance that the world will end within your lifetime? Not that your own little world will end—that the mess in your bedroom will spontaneously combust or that you'll fall asleep in school from boredom and never wake up—but that the whole planet will go up in smoke? What if what waits for you just around the corner of life is nothing less than the *grand finale* of planetary history?

The Big Bad Moment

The new millennium is big stuff. It's a *mood*—a whole upcoming decade. It's a *moment*—the blink in time of one New Year's Eve. And it's guaranteed to make a *memory*—an imprint on the brain of anyone alive enough to watch a clock tick as it enters. Never mind that people don't agree when the new millennium starts—whether it's 2000 or 2001—and that either year is just a mark on an arbitrary human calendar. Or that parts of the planet don't even reckon time by our calendar. The millennium is like a cosmic stranger who slaps you and says, "Excuse me. I'd like to interrupt your destiny."

Some say the new millennium will bring nothing but good—a *bloomsday* for the human race. But a big chunk of people say it will bring nothing but evil. Ultimate bad. Total *doomsday*. Many Christians look around and say that the world is getting darker. There's more sin. Evil political leaders. Rampaging ungodliness, moral ugliness, and untruth. Schools that brainwash youth into political correctness. And looking at these and other "signs of the end times," they predict three things will happen soon, likely *within your lifetime if not the next decade*:

1. *The Rapture of the church.* Jesus will come again to earth to whisk away those who know him to eternal safety.

2. *The rise of the Antichrist.* The Beast—think of him as the man who wants to put a 666 brand on your hand—will establish a one-world government, economy, and religion united in hatred of God.

3. *A time of Great Tribulation.* Anyone left behind at Christ's return will face a torturous existence as God pours

out his wrath on the planet.

Here's a taste of what they say:

- "We are the terminal generation," says John Hagee in his New York Times bestseller *Beginning of the End*. More than half a million copies of his book leave no doubt: the world will end in our generation.
- Grant Jeffrey writes in *Price of Darkness: Antichrist and the New World Order* that "The world is moving relentlessly toward its final crisis . . . those who place their faith in Christ know this crisis will culminate in the return of Jesus the Messiah."
- *Left Behind* is a survival manual written specifically "for those who will remain *after* the rapture" (that is, for those left behind after Christ returns). Author Peter Lalonde says in another book that we are "racing toward the mark of the beast." Still another Lalonde book says "the final countdown has begun" and offers "clear evidence that we are, without a doubt, standing on the edge of time."
- The novel *Left Behind* (sound familiar?) and its sequel, *Tribulation Force*, detail life after Christ's return. Co-author Tim LaHaye says in another book, *When the Trumpet Sounds*, that he sees twelve signs that show Christ's second coming is likely to happen soon.
- In *2001: On the Edge of Eternity*, Jack Van Impe "spells out the details of end-time prophecy, showing with pinpoint clarity how the 'signs of the times' and the 'end of the age' spoken of by Jesus Christ are being revealed before our eyes." Based on his "six-day theory" of history, he predicts that the world will end between the years 2000 and 2012.

Countless other books, tapes, videos, and radio and TV programs say more of the same: *This is the beginning of the*

13

end. The last of the world as we know it. For cats, dogs, and people. Christian and non. For everyone.

Really? Now?

Maybe. Or maybe not.

Jesus is coming back real soon—like by the year 2000, they say, *or even before—or soon after.*

Someday? For sure. The Bible is clear.

In the next few years?

Maybe. Or maybe not.

Your Freakish World

In case you've missed it, there *are* freaky things happening in your world. They're world-stopping changes we never saw coming: The Oklahoma City bombing. David Koresh. The Aum Shinrikyo cult stockpiling Nazi-invented nerve gas—and wafting it through Japan's subway system. Nuclear weapons loose in Russia (complete with a Russian parliament reluctant to ratify arms-reduction treaties). AIDS, the Ebola virus, flesh-eating bacteria, and mad cow disease. Weapons of mass destruction—even chemicals and germs that kill without going *boom*. Abortion, addiction, pollution, overpopulation, and desertification. Global warming—or maybe a new ice age.

But you don't have to read the newspaper to fill up on bad news. Sit in a hospital waiting room and witness the fear and anger of daily personal tragedies. Look around—maybe at your own family—to understand what "the destruction of the nuclear family" is all about.

And there's the grind of everyday sickness, overwork, tough classes, and friends who go stupid on you. Not to mention that rude reality of high school graduation that launches you into a real-world fight for survival.

However you define your "world"—your innards, your family, your community, your country, your globe—you're likely to see a world of hurt. It can feel like you're chained to the wall of a dungeon—and people are zinging knives at you.

Reading the Future

Two out of five teens are in a sour mood right now—and a high percentage of teens are more than a little pessimistic. Since you were a little kid it's seemed like the world has been getting weirder and worser—building toward a crisis like a whopper zit coming to a head. The planet feels explosive, ready to erupt.

What will your future look like?

Can you control what happens?

Is the future that awaits you good or bad?

Who wins? Who loses? Who's toast?

Who can you trust?

What's going to end your world?

Is there any hope?

Fair questions. The answers matter more than a little. If the world really *is* ending so soon, what kind of life are you going to live? Will you choose a career? Why go to college if the world will close down sometime next year—or before you have a chance to use your education? Will you get married? Have kids? Your life plans surely will take a different turn if you don't plan to exist in 2005—or 2050. Why think about tomorrow if tomorrow doesn't exist? Why not max out your parents' plastic—and then pray for Jesus to come before the bill does? Why not go live in a commune and wait for aliens to arrive?

Believe it or don't, plenty of people have shattered their lives because they were sure Jesus would come back pronto—as in *no way no how* are they wrong about his quick arrival. But there's a flip side to that reality: You could also easily undo your life if you convince yourself Jesus is *never* coming back.

What you think about the future will make you careful or crazy, hopeful or depressed—and it's a greased slide from depression to despair to desperation. *Waaah! Watch out!*

The Ultimate End

You have a life to live—you hope. Will the world have time for you?

One answer is to say, "Fret not. The world won't ever end. Christ? He's a myth. His return is a hoax. Live long and prosper. Ignore all of this and it will go away."

Another answer is what you'll hear more and more: "The world will end today. Or tomorrow. At the very least, before you grow old. We know with certainty that Christ is coming soon, that we are living in the 'end times.' Prepare for the end. Borrow money for a burrito today because you won't be around to pay it back tomorrow."

Maybe there's a different answer.

The Bible *does* say a lot about the future. Jesus *did* promise to come back to take those of us who know him to his Father's mansion. God *will* either convert or conquer evildoers, and in the process rescue believers to himself. He *wants* to give us insight into our future that enables us to cope with life's sometimes-harsh present. But *when* his coming will take place—he said only his Father in heaven knows (Matthew 24:36).

Your reaction can take extremes. "This is a crock." Or you might think, "This message rocks."

It's your right to guess. Go ahead and lay odds. Ladies and gents, place your bets.

Guess wrong and you might *wallow* in the end, wasting time and energy waiting for an end to life that may not come in your lifetime. Guess wrong and you could *accelerate* the end, letting your brain be vacuumed out of your head and taking a cultish ride on a comet. Or guess wrong and you might *ignore* the end, missing out on truths about the future that affect your life today.

What does the future really hold? Who knows? Who really knows?

You can't ignore what's going on around you. You have to figure it out—and find out what your future looks like.

In the year 1999 and seven months
the great King of Terror
will come from the sky.
He will bring back to life
the great king of the Mongols.
Before and after war reigns
happily unrestrained.

Nostradamus (1503-1566)
French physician and astrologer
Century X, quatrain 72

2

Living on the Edge of the End

It's the freakiest stuff you'll ever read—the Bible's prophecies describing what will happen at the end of time:

- *A rash of disasters.* "You will hear of wars and rumors of wars. . . . Nation will rise against nation, and kingdom against kingdom. There will be famines and earthquakes in various places" (Matthew 24:6–7).
- *The Beastly 666.* "[The beast's sidekick] also forced everyone, small and great, rich and poor, free and slave, to receive a mark on his right hand or on his forehead, so that no one could buy or sell unless he had the mark, which is the name of the beast or the number of his name . . . 666" (Revelation 13:16–18).
- *Seven years of horrors in the Great Tribulation.* An example: "A third of mankind was killed by the three plagues of fire, smoke and sulfur that came out of their mouths. The power of the horses was in their mouths and in their tails; for their tails were like snakes, having heads with which they inflict injury" (Revelation 9:18–19).

- *Christ's dazzling second coming.* "The Son of Man will appear in the sky, and all the nations of the earth will mourn. They will see the Son of Man coming on the clouds of the sky, with power and great glory. And he will send his angels with a loud trumpet call, and they will gather his elect from the four winds, from one end of the heavens to the other" (Matthew 24:30–31).
- *The destiny of Christians.* "For the Lord himself will come down from heaven, with a loud command, with the voice of the archangel and with the trumpet call of God, and the dead in Christ will rise first. After that, we who are still alive and are left will be caught up with them in the clouds to meet the Lord in the air. And so we will be with the Lord forever" (1 Thessalonians 4:16–17).
- *The demise of Satan.* "And the devil, who deceived them, was thrown into the lake of burning sulfur, where the beast and the false prophet had been thrown. They will be tormented day and night for ever and ever" (Revelation 20:10).

Two thousand years ago a one-of-a-kind baby appeared in Bethlehem. Jesus was born human, but he was more than that. He was the Son of God, who grew up to die for our sins. And he rose from the dead—proving his identity and confirming the success of his mission. While Christians argue over the details of what will take place when the world dies, they agree on the main points: Jesus will appear a second time—and this time not as a helpless baby but as all-powerful Lord of all. He will crush evildoers. He will establish his eternal kingdom. And he will take Christians home to live with him forever.

We Are Not Alone

Christian writers, preachers, and other leaders see signs that all these events will take place *soon*—if not before. Yet

Christians aren't the only people saying that humankind is trudging a rocky road, dodging boulders and booby traps. While Christians believe the Bible best spells out the *who-what-when-where-how* of the end, there are countless visions of the end of time that don't have God in the plot line.

Scientists from a variety of fields, for example, spot endless dangers about to bonk the world:

- That one-in-ten-thousand chance that *a comet or asteroid will plow into earth* in your lifetime has astronomers discussing ways to blast that unwanted space junk to bits.
- A long-term *decrease in the earth's magnetic field* has others warning of a deadly increase in cosmic radiation—though we probably have hundreds of years to fix the problem or make a Supermanish exit from the planet.
- *Global warming* will bring the earth to a boil, according to yet another group. But don't hurry to buy soon-to-be-beachfront property in Saskatchewan. Some say global warming will flood the coasts, increase precipitation, and touch off an ice age that could put us all under miles of snow. They also say that radical climate shifts may take place in as little as two or three years. Better get to DisneyWorld before it goes snow white.

Politicians, conservationists, and other activists let you take your pick from several other looming catastrophes:

- *Nuclear weapons.* The Cold War between the United States and the former Soviet Union is over. But the "new world order" has created multiple nasty scenarios. We're left with *terrorist organizations* and *rogue nations* who will *build* and/or *buy* weapons for use in *blackmail* or *traditional warfare.*

21

- *Deforestation.* Clearing rain forests not only contributes to global warming but destroys the habitats of millions of plant and animal species. Are *you* the next specimen scheduled for extinction?
- *Desertification.* Countless acres around the world have been overused to the point that they won't grow a weed—much less sprout corn or feed a cow. The result? Dust bowls and deserts.
- *Overpopulation.* The world hasn't adapted to *5.8 billion* people crawling its surface. How will we function with *11 billion* cramming into the same space by the year 2050? Prepare to share.
- *Pollution.* Pesticides and herbicides, industrial and consumer waste foul air, water, and land. By some counts, you produce twice your weight in waste every day.

If that brief list doesn't depress you, you can catch an update on all things threatening the existence of humankind by dialing 1–415–673–DOOM. (Anyone else notice that "OOM" on the phone pad is 666? *Spooky.*) As the "Society for Secular Armageddonism" sees it, *people* are the ones bringing on earth's total destruction. They name "human conceit, violence, greed, and bigotry" as the four major threats to the planet—the "four horsemen of the secular apocalypse." It's a wacky parallel to God's four horsemen of Revelation 6:1–8. "God isn't involved here," they say, "this being a purely do-it-yourself apocalypse."

Just Hold Your Horsemen!

Time out!

Here's the big problem: Saying something is true doesn't mean it is. And here's the big question: Do these predictions—by people Christian and non—signal a coming-soon-to-a-neighborhood-near-you end of the world?

Take a lesson from TV.

How so?

Amaze your friends with this factoid: There are only about five or six sitcom plots in existence in the whole known universe. Weekly episodes of your favorite shows regurgitate endless flavors of these same five or six plots. There's BOY MEETS GIRL (where boy and girl usually have a fight, make up, and live happily ever after—at least until the end of the episode). There's the MY PARENTS ARE GOING TO KILL ME IF THEY FIND OUT plot. Surely you've seen the FLASHBACK DREAM. (Normally, producers recycle material *they* know you've seen but *you* don't. In the FLASHBACK DREAM they reheat leftovers even *you* know you've met before.)

You can figure out the one or two other stock plots yourself. But one more classic is the LOST CHARACTERS plot. You've seen it everywhere from *Winnie the Pooh* to *Home Improvement* to *Gilligan's Island*—a perpetual LOST CHARACTER plot. Characters wander and wonder in circles, sooner or later arriving back at the same spot they started. It goes on and on and on and on and . . .

Been There, Done That—Predictions That Have Failed

Not to burst any bubbles, but when it comes to predicting the swift and immediate end of the world, we've been here before. The human race—and yes, Christians—are going around in circles. We're coming back to a spot we've already seen. It's a cosmic case of *been there, done that*.

Not long ago a book predicted that 65 million Americans would soon starve to death. Famine would spread from coast to coast as the population of the United States outstripped the land's capacity to produce food.

The prediction was made in Paul Ehrlich's *The Population Bomb*. Publication date? 1968. When was America supposed to starve to death? The 1980s.

Reports of the death of the planet were greatly exaggerated. *You* are living proof Ehrlich was wrong.

It would take a far fatter book than this to examine the true threat of asteroid collisions, nuclear terrorism, and environmental disasters. But watch out for this: Even scientists fudge facts. Scientific claims need scientific support. So study up before you get scared.

Here's the point: Just because someone says something is true doesn't mean it is. So just because Christians say the end of the world is coming pronto doesn't mean you should believe them. Look back at just a few of the botched predictions well known in church history. There's oodles more:

- A.D. 156—*The Montanist Movement*. Montanus and his followers claimed that they'd had wild experiences of God and Technicolor visions. They preached that the New Jerusalem was about to descend from the sky to land in Turkey. Even the most famous theologian in the West of the time, Tertullian, joined in. (These guys and girls weren't connected to all those militias roaming Montana, by the way.)
- A.D. 1000—*The Great Big Doomsday Party*. Around 900 A.D., a council of the church announced that humanity was entering the last century of history. As the end of 999 drew near, people all across Europe donated their homes and possessions to the poor. Prisoners and farm animals scampered free. Thousands of Christians flocked to Jerusalem, drawn to the spot where they thought Jesus would come down on the clouds. One account says that as Pope Sylvester II celebrated mass

to a standing-room-only crowd at St. Peter's Basilica in Rome, "not a few [died] from fright, giving up their ghosts then and there." At midnight the bells pealed wildly. And we're still here to tell about it.

- A.D. 1260—*Joachim of Fiore*. This Italian monk preached that the Antichrist was already alive. Others stretched his teachings even further, claiming that the Pope himself was the Antichrist and priests his evil partners.
- A.D. 1527—A German bookbinder named *Hans Nut*— fitting, huh?—proclaimed he was a prophet of God. He said Christ would arrive in 1528 to usher in a thousand years of free food and free sex. Herr Nut was captured and later killed in an attempted prison break.
- A.D. 1533—In another flare-up of end-time expectation, the Anabaptist *Jan Matthys* gathered a group of revolutionary followers to aid him in speeding Christ's return by force. He became the big cheese in Münster, Germany, expelling all Lutherans and Catholics. He turned polygamist, confiscated property, and stashed weapons. A David Koresh prequel.
- A.D. 1842—In upstate New York, *William Miller and the "Millerites"* preached that Christ would return in 1843. In 1844, four wrong dates later, what had become a loud and large movement collapsed. Miller eventually admitted his error and died a broken man.
- A.D. 1914—and 1915, 1918, 1923, 1925, and 1975—the *Jehovah's Witnesses* have yet to hit it right with their predictions of the end.

Maybe you shrug: *People sure were stupid way back when.*

Not so fast. You don't have to look back to the darkish middle ages or to a faraway land or to off-the-wall religious movements to discover feverish, false predictions that Jesus would return soon.

Those Crazy Christians

The 1960s seemed like ancient history until Bill Clinton became president. Everyone longed for the groovy days of John F. Kennedy, the Beatles invasion, and Woodstock. Hippie stuff got hip again.

Your parents would probably rather forget the 1970s. But polyester and other fake fibers have sprung back to life. Disco is stayin' alive. Even Barry "I Am Music and I Write the Songs" Manilow is allowed back on television. And the BeeGees are now honored members of the Rock and Roll Hall of Fame.

The near-past isn't as way back as it sometimes feels. In the grand scheme of things, in fact, the 1980s are practically yesterday. Maybe it's the decade you were born.

Want to know what *really* went on in the '80s?

We, the high school graduating class of 1982, spent our teenhood watching movies like *The Day After* (a made-for-TV movie depicting life after thermonuclear war) and *War Games* (where Matthew Broderick hacks into the U.S. Department of Defense and almost makes the world go *ka-blooey*). In social studies we watched the 1950s civil defense flick *Duck and Cover*. The film said that if we saw a bright flash we should jump under our desks—or snuggle under a picnic blanket. We laughed. We knew better. It would be *ka-flash*, *ka-boom*, and *ka-burn*, more or less all at once.

The news media said America was losing the arms race to the Soviet Union—and that the United States would be wiped out during a "window of vulnerability" in the 1980s. Many people protested for a "nuclear freeze" (no new nu-warheads) or even "unilateral disarmament" (we de-nukes in hope that the Soviet Union would destroy theirs), but the 1980s instead brought a colossal arms race. Though that costly phase of the Cold War eventually blew the Soviet Union apart, we didn't foresee that. We went to bed counting the missiles pointed at us. We debated whether it would be better to be bomb droppings or to survive and live in nuclear winter.

It gets weirder.

Many Christians thought these and other dire predictions signaled that Christ would return at any moment. We asked our parents why we should go to school or college if the world wouldn't be here when we grew up. We watched end-times movies in church basements—Christian films like *Thief in the Night* and *Distant Thunder*—that scared the BAJEEBERS out of us. (Both are still HOT rentals at many Christian bookstores.)

It wasn't so long ago. We weren't doing drugs. And we weren't stupid.

Hang tight. It gets even weirder:

- A.D. 1988—*Edgar Whisenaut* wrote *88 Reasons Why the Rapture Will Be in 1988* to tell the world that Jesus would return in September 1988. His revised edition set the date for October 3, 1989. Needless to say, we're all still waiting for *99 Reasons Why the Rapture Will Be in 1999*. Or *10 Reasons for 2010*.

- A.D. 1992—*Lee Jang Rim* of Korea ignited widespread panic both in Korea and parts of the United States when he predicted Christ would return on October 28, 1992. Many of Lee's followers sold belongings and resigned jobs. Four committed suicide. On the predicted night, a thousand followers gathered in Lee's church to wait for the *hyoo-go* (rapture) to occur. Fifteen hundred riot police waited outside. Church leaders were beaten by those who felt duped. Lee faced fraud charges.

- A.D. 1993—*David Koresh* proclaimed he was Christ come again. When government agents rammed holes into the Waco, Texas, compound of Koresh's Branch Davidians and shot tear gas inside, Koresh died with seventy-five or more of his followers, including some twenty children. Many victims burned to death in fires apparently set by the Branch Davidians; others were shot in the head. Koresh had predicted he and his followers were fulfilling biblical prophecies that God would judge his enemies by fire.
- A.D. 1994—*Harold Camping*, well-known owner of a large network of Christian radio stations, predicted Christ would return between September 15 and 27. Still here reading? Thought so. Camping's explanation? He miscounted.

While these stories range from the pitiful to the scary, once again, you're living proof. They were wrong.

What's the Real Story?

Throughout history people have claimed to have the scoop on God's schedule for End of the World Day. They're way off. Totally wrong. All of them.

They're confused about *who's coming*. Is it David Koresh? Jan Matthys? Or will it be the true Jesus of Scripture?

They're confused about *what will happen*. A pizza bash? Polygamy? Jerusalem docking with earth like an overgrown Mir space station?

And they're confused about *when it will happen*. Will it be A.D. 156? The year 2525? Or any date in between?

Today's preachers point out that just because those date-setters of the past were wrong doesn't mean *they* are. On that technicality of logic, they're correct.

Some today say they've spotted the Antichrist. Others

say they've unlocked the signs of the times. All say they've seen the beginning of the end.

Maybe they're right.

Maybe not.

"I'm not saying we are Jesus.
It's nothing as beautiful
but it is almost as big....
We have found out, baby,
we have this mission
before coming into this life....
All I will say is it's in the Bible
in *Revelation*."

Marshall "Do" Applewhite (1932-1997)
Leader of the Heaven's Gate cult
Time, April 7, 1997

3

The Bopponauts Missed Their Spaceboat

Members of the Heaven's Gate cult had seemed like quiet, clean-cut, vaguely Christian computer nerds. When they laced up their new Nikes, shed their bodily "containers" in group suicide, and tried to soar to a higher existence on a spaceship said to trail Comet Hale-Bopp, we caught up with what the Bopponauts really believed.

Heaven's Gaters used a load of Christian terms, but their version of Jesus and their vision of the end sounded nothing like the Bible. They taught that two thousand years ago the "Kingdom Level Above Human" appointed a representative—a being who inhabited the container called "Jesus"—to preach the kingdom of God to earthlings. When Jesus died, Applewhite and his partner were appointed in his place. They were the sole "shepherds" who could lead humans to a higher level of life. The couple we now know as "Do and Ti" even claimed to be the two witnesses Revelation says would appear just prior to the end of the world.

The Heaven's Gaters promised a spacecraft would swoop down for anyone who joined them—joined them through suicide, that is, preferably from the southwestern United

States. (You gotta wonder why just the southwest. To save space gas?) The press release they left behind told how: "The requirement is to not only believe who the Representatives are, but, *to do as they and we did. . . .* This includes the ultimate sacrifice and demonstration of faith—that is, *the shedding of your human body.* You must call on the name of TI and DO to assist you. In so doing, you will engage a communication of sorts, alerting a spacecraft to your location where you will be picked up after shedding your vehicle, and taken to another world—by members of the Kingdom of Heaven" (italics added; http://www.heavensgate.org/misc/pressrel.htm).

Don't try that at home. It was a limited-time offer.

The Kingdom Level Above Human?

Jesus *did* talk all the time about the kingdom of Heaven. But what he described sounded nothing like "the Kingdom Level Above Human." The eleventh chapter of Revelation *does* describe two witnesses who appear during the end times. But they're representatives of the God of the universe, not a petty galactic council. They proclaim Christ, the one true Shepherd. And there was no saucer-flying Scotty waiting to beam up the Heaven's Gaters.

Applewhite got it wrong.

Joachim of Fiore, Hans Nut, William Miller, David Koresh, and plenty of others got it wrong too—each deceived in a different way.

If the Bible is so unclear that people can't keep the story line straight, why study it at all? Why bother to figure out what it says? Why use the Bible to peer into the future?

Because God made forward-looking prophecy some of the major stuff of the Bible.

Because his words are worth our trust.

And because in the Bible God makes the major points of future history unmistakably clear.

God is no hermit. He specializes in showing us who he is. Creation leaves no doubt about his existence and character: "The heavens declare the glory of God; the skies proclaim the work of his hands" (Psalm 19:1). God came to us in human flesh in Jesus, putting his utter perfection on display for all to see: "He [Jesus] is the image of the invisible God" (Colossians 1:15). And through his prime spokesfolks—the Old Testament prophets, Jesus, and the New Testament writers—God lets us glimpse humanity's ultimate fate. He tells us what the world and his kingdom will look like at the end of time.

And here's what makes the Bible believable: This tell-the-future thing is nothing new for God. In fact, we dare to use the Bible as a guidebook to what's ahead because the Bible *already* has a long record of predictions—biblical prophecies—that came true. It's proof unmatched by any other source of knowledge about the future.

Up Your Nostradamus

Smart people can peek into the future—but that doesn't make them prophets. The info you need to take a stab at the stock market, blizzard forecasts, and the Vikings' chances of ever winning a Super Bowl can be gleaned from corporate reports, Doppler radar, and team stats. Eggheads can guess good, but their insight is way less than flawless. Stocks take surprise dives, snowstorms go south, and big wishes don't win bowl games. There's a massive difference between these people—call them *predictors* or *prognosticators*—and the men and women the Bible calls *prophets*—people God appoints and enables to speak for him.

The Bible's prophets were unique in *what they talked*

about. They prophesied about Israel, and often about neighboring nations. They spoke judgment and encouragement, telling about God's rules and grace and his plan for a relationship with the planet he'd made. Often prophets spoke to their own times, but sometimes they disclosed the future. They foretold the Messiah—a hero-to-come who would save not only God's special people, Israel, but the whole world. And they saw clear to the end of time.

The Bible's prophets were also unique in *how they spoke.* The Bible boldly claims to be far more than a few thousand years' worth of shrink-wrapped human wisdom. It records the words of God himself, uttered through his prophets:

- God put his words in the mouth of prophets and commanded them to speak his full message (Deuteronomy 18:18).
- God inspired his prophets to speak *his* mind, not their own: "No prophecy of Scripture came about by the prophet's own interpretation. For prophecy never had its origin in the will of man, but men spoke from God as they were carried along by the Holy Spirit" (2 Peter 1:20–21).
- God expected his people to heed the words of the prophet as coming from God himself: "If anyone does not listen to my words that the prophet speaks in my name, I myself will call him to account" (Deuteronomy 18:19).

God speaking through his prophets is kind of like your mom or dad sending you a message through your little sister. You might be able to squash your sister, but you'd still better obey the message she brings as a word from on high.

God expected his people to take prophecy, well, *seriously.* They were to sift through messages and ignore misspoken words (Deuteronomy 18:21–22). They were even to kill any prophet who garbled the message. A prophet who didn't tell the truth or predicted the future apart from God's inspiration risked being found false—and becoming target practice for a stoning squad (Deuteronomy 18:20).

Probably not a standard of perfection you want your teachers to apply to your next oral report.

Unlike occult prophets like Nostradamus, who uttered his predictions with all the clarity of fortune cookies, God's prophets foretold the future in mind-boggling specifics. And unlike money managers and meteorologists, these true prophets of God produced a perfect record of rightness we can all profit from. Their clear predictions about Christ are evidence that we can trust the Bible's prophecies. Hundreds of years before Christ lived, died, and rose from the dead, the Bible's writers told us all about him. Check out ten amazing samples:

Ten Prophecies About Christ and Their Fulfillment

1. Christ would be born to a virgin

Prophecy: "Therefore the Lord himself will give you a sign: The virgin will be with child and will give birth to a son, and will call him Immanuel" (Isaiah 7:14).

Prophecy Fulfilled: " 'The virgin will be with child and will give birth to a son, and they will call him Immanuel'—which means, 'God with us' " (Matthew 1:23).

2. Christ would be born to the family line of King David

Prophecy: "For to us a child is born, to us a son is given, and the government will be on his shoulders. And he will be called Wonderful Counselor, Mighty God, Everlasting

Father, Prince of Peace. Of the increase of his government and peace there will be no end. He will reign on David's throne and over his kingdom, establishing and upholding it with justice and righteousness from that time on and forever. The zeal of the LORD Almighty will accomplish this" (Isaiah 9:6–7).

Prophecy Fulfilled: "David was the father of Solomon ... and Jacob the father of Joseph, the husband of Mary, of whom was born Jesus, who is called Christ" (Matthew 1:6, 16).

3. Christ would be born in Bethlehem

Prophecy: " 'But you, Bethlehem Ephrathah, though you are small among the clans of Judah, out of you will come for me one who will be ruler over Israel, whose origins are from of old, from ancient times' " (Micah 5:2).

Prophecy Fulfilled: "After Jesus was born in Bethlehem in Judea, during the time of King Herod, Magi from the east came to Jerusalem" (Matthew 2:1).

4. The birth of Christ would be announced by a star

Prophecy: "I see him, but not now; I behold him, but not near. A star will come out of Jacob; a scepter will rise out of Israel. He will crush the foreheads of Moab, the skulls of all the sons of Sheth" (Numbers 24:17).

Prophecy Fulfilled: "After Jesus was born in Bethlehem in Judea, during the time of King Herod, Magi from the east came to Jerusalem and asked, 'Where is the one who has been born king of the Jews? We saw his star in the east and have come to worship him' " (Matthew 2:1–2).

5. Christ would do miracles

Prophecy: "Then will the eyes of the blind be opened and the ears of the deaf unstopped. Then will the lame leap like a deer, and the tongue of the dumb shout for joy. Water will gush forth in the wilderness and streams in the desert" (Isaiah 35:5–6).

Prophecy
Fulfilled: "Jesus went through all the towns and villages, teaching in their synagogues, preaching the good news of the kingdom and healing every disease and sickness" (Matthew 9:35).

6. A friend would betray Christ

Prophecy: "Even my close friend, whom I trusted, he who shared my bread, has lifted up his heel against me" (Psalm 41:9).

Prophecy
Fulfilled: " 'I am telling you now before it happens, so that when it does happen you will believe that I am He.' After he had said this, Jesus was troubled in spirit and testified, 'I tell you the truth, one of you is going to betray me' " (John 13:19, 21).

7. Christ's hands and feet would be pierced

Prophecy: "Dogs have surrounded me; a band of evil men has encircled me, they have pierced my hands and my feet" (Psalm 22:16).

Prophecy
Fulfilled: "When they came to the place called The Skull, there they crucified him, along with the criminals—one on his right, the other on his left" (Luke 23:33).

8. Christ's clothes would be divided and lots would be cast for them

Prophecy: "They divide my garments among them and cast lots for my clothing" (Psalm 22:18).

Prophecy
Fulfilled: "When the soldiers crucified Jesus, they took his clothes, dividing them into four shares, one for each of them, with the undergarment remaining. This garment was seamless, woven in one piece from top to bottom. 'Let's not tear it,' they said to one another. 'Let's decide by lot who will get it' " (John 19:23–24).

9. Christ would rise from the dead

Prophecy: "... because you will not abandon me to the grave, nor will you let your Holy One see decay" (Psalm 16:10).

Prophecy Fulfilled: " 'Don't be alarmed,' he said. 'You are looking for Jesus the Nazarene, who was crucified. He has risen! He is not here. See the place where they laid him' " (Mark 16:6).

10. Christ would ascend to heaven

Prophecy: "When you ascended on high, you led captives in your train; you received gifts from men, even from the rebellious—that you, O LORD God, might dwell there" (Psalm 68:18).

Prophecy Fulfilled: "After he said this, he was taken up before their very eyes, and a cloud hid him from their sight" (Acts 1:9).

Amazing examples—and these are only a handful of the scads of biblical prophecies already fulfilled. Not only do they demonstrate Christ's unique identity as God's Son, but they also validate the reliability of the Bible's views of the future.

Put it this way. If a friend constantly tells lies, you stop believing her. If a friend has a habit of telling the truth, you learn she's worth trusting. But if a friend could tell the truth perfectly—with total knowledge of all things and with complete accuracy—you'd have reason to trust her completely. The Bible is like that friend.

Trust—and Understanding

Here's the problem: You can *trust* the Bible—yet still *misunderstand* it. You can dare to use the Bible because of its reliability. But you'll only get what the Bible means if

you're careful how you interpret it. You're bound to become nuts if you
 read more than is there
 read less than is there
 focus on itty bitty issues and miss the big ones.
Here's the truth: Bible prophecy isn't quite as ready-to-read as a road map. The details aren't always as straightforward to figure out as we'd like. Yet three quick reading rules can help us keep the main points of the Bible straight.

Rule One: Read to Obey

Our society is on info overload. By ten o'clock in the morning you're exposed to more information than previous generations ever thunk up. You're assaulted by music ... videos ... internet blabber ... broken promises ... bald lies. The hard drive in your head screams DISK FULL, and you flip off your brain.

To live in your world is to shut up and shut out. Yet you know it's stupid not to listen up
 ... when a teacher says, "This is going to be on the test."
 ... when a parent says, "Be home by midnight or else."
 ... when a judge says, "One more ticket and you'll lose your license."

At times like those you know to listen—or face a *heap-a-trouble*.

Jesus tells us to grab hold of his truth and test it. He promises that those who try it out will confirm its truthfulness (John 8:31–32). God even makes a specific promise to those who hear and heed the words of the Bible book of Revelation: "Behold, I am coming soon! Blessed is he who *keeps* the words of the prophecy in this book" (italics added; Revelation 22:7).

Rule Two: Read What It Actually Says

A quick example of how *not* to read the Bible: Acts 1:9–11 says, "After he [Jesus] said this, he was taken up before their very eyes, and a cloud hid him from their sight. They were looking intently up into the sky as he was going, when suddenly two men dressed in white stood beside them. 'Men of Galilee,' they said, 'why do you stand here looking into the sky? This same Jesus, who has been taken from you into heaven, will come back in the same way you have seen him go into heaven.' "

It would be easy to invent explanations of Jesus' ascension to heaven. A stunt man says it was strings and wires. A psychologist says the crowd hallucinated *en masse*. A Trekkie says a spaceship was hiding in the clouds.

Toss all three theories. The people of New Testament times knew the difference between the natural and the miraculous, between mechanical and golly-wow-how-did-that-happen events. Our human explanations aren't in the text—because they aren't what occurred. The author of Acts, Luke, a doctor aiming to accurately record the *history* of Jesus' time on earth (Luke 1:1–4), says that Jesus was simply "taken up."

When we read the Bible we can't add to it. Heaven's Gaters taught that "The only time that Next Kingdom can be entered is when there is a Member or Members of that Kingdom [that is, Applewhite] who have come into the human kingdom, incarnated as we have, offering clarification of that information" (http://www.heavensgate.org/misc/intro.htm).

It's easy to preach fuzzy ideas about "God" or "heaven." But the Bible is clear on what those terms mean. It tells us what heaven is like—and how we get there *only* through Jesus (John 14:6). Jesus said, "Here I am! I stand at the door and knock. If anyone hears my voice and opens the door, I will come in and eat with him, and he with me" (Revelation 3:20). Heaven's Gaters *added* the message that no one could enter heaven without Marshall Applewhite's help.

When we read the Bible we can't take away from it. Another example from Applewhite: He laughed that Christians could "graciously accept death with the hope that 'through His shed blood,' or some other equally worthless religious precept, you will go to Heaven after your death" (http://www.heavensgate.org/misc/intro.htm). Applewhite attempted to strip away Jesus' unique identity as the Son of God, the substitute who died in our place.

Don't you hate it when friends interrupt—and chop off what you wanted to say? Isn't it annoying when people finish your sentences—and bang their own thoughts into yours? You want people to understand all your words. The Bible deserves the same respect.

When we read the Bible we study hard. God acted to compose the Bible over several centuries. His thoughts are recorded in a variety of—don't gag—literary forms. In the New Testament, for example, Jesus *lectured* his followers, Paul wrote *letters* to churches and to individuals. John had a *vision* he recorded as Revelation in a written form similar to other Jewish books of the time—what Bible scholars call *apocalyptic literature.* In any modern library, apocalyptic literature would be shelved in the Spooky and Hard-to-Understand section—it's got trumpets and bowls of wrath and six-winged creatures covered with eyes all around. But any real reading of the Bible respects the qualities it possesses as a book—language, context, culture, authorship. Maybe you can fib your way through English essay tests with made-up interpretations of books. Don't bluff your way through the Bible.

Rule Three: Read for the Big Stuff

It's possible to build an entire mis-religion on a single misunderstanding of the Bible. One final Applewhite-ism: "In Heaven there are—there will be—no males and no females (it is genderless). It is not a mammalian existence, it is not a human existence. And those documents also clearly tell you that you have to leave everything of the human world in order to know that Next World or ever see that Kingdom of Heaven" (http:// www.heavensgate.org/misc/vt092996.htm).

Applewhite had focused the sum of his teaching on a goofed read of Galatians 3:26–28: "You are all sons of God through faith in Christ Jesus, for all of you who were baptized into Christ have clothed yourselves with Christ. There is neither Jew nor Greek, slave nor free, male nor female, for you are all one in Christ Jesus." Paul wrote those words as a clear statement of the equality of men and women in Christ. The Heaven's Gaters misread this passage—and wound up a nut-hut of shaved heads and neutered men. Yikes!

The full sweep of the Bible tells us one thing—that the purpose of all God's acts throughout all the universe is for us to come to know him through Jesus: "Salvation is found in no one else, for there is no other name under heaven given to men by which we must be saved" (Acts 4:12). Even studying Bible prophecy can make you major on minors— if you let that *fraction* of faith push aside the rest. ("It's fine that Jesus died to save us," smarms one well-known prophecy figure, "BUT THANK GOD FOR BIBLE PROPHECY.") Easy test: Any vision of the future or theory of God that misses or misshapes or minimizes Jesus is automatically wrong.

42

A Sure Promise—Plus Some Fuzzy Details

The Bible's words about the end of the world both shake and soothe. Jesus said, "Do not let your hearts be troubled. Trust in God; trust also in me. In my Father's house are many rooms; if it were not so, I would have told you. I am going there to prepare a place for you. And if I go and prepare a place for you, I will come back and take you to be with me that you also may be where I am" (John 14:1–3).

Jesus is coming again for his people.

His promise is clear.

It's some of the details that get fuzzy.

God gave us the Bible to peer into the future. Its prophecies are trustworthy. And it makes the big points of future history unmistakably clear.

So let's sneak some peeks at the future of your world.

Man's extremity is God's opportunity.

John Flavel (1630-1691)
English evangelist and author
*A Faithful and Ancient Account of Some
Late and Wonderful Sea Deliverances*

4

This Means War

Here's an experiment. Rip open a bag of chips. Pour half into a bowl. Feed that half to your dog or your dad. Or spill them on the floor. Now look at the bag of chips. Hold it. Study it. Turn it around. And upside down—only if you clipped it shut. Profound question: Is the bag of chips you hold in your hands half full or half empty?

Half full! You still own 2.5 football games worth of eats—assuming you don't share and don't inhale chips whole. Or enough for 4.6 after-school minisnacks.

Half empty! You can't make the missing half come back. You can't pretend those chips are still there. And you can never claim half a bag is better than a whole.

Don't cry over spilled chips. Life has bigger problems. After all, the bag is just a picture of the world you live in.

Look around. You see a mess of good and bad. It's a world half full and half empty:

Chubby babies—and hungry children.

Sunsets—and smog.

Wedding bells—and divorce court.

Dogs—and cats. Or is it cats—and rats?

Peace—and war.

Fridays—and Mondays.

Airbags—and mangled metal.

Great teachers—and hideous you-know-who at your school.

Life is a jumble. *Disappointment. Hope. Violence. Safety. Fear. Courage. Rage. Calm. Hatred. Love. Grief. Joy.* Good is God and friends and family. Good is chocolate and graham crackers and marshmallow melting together to make you want s'more. Bad is the bully who likes to pound your face. When his arm is cocked, ready to bash your nose—time stops. You think, *It isn't supposed to be this way.*

Flashback to Paradise

It *wasn't* always this way. Once upon a time the bag was stuffed full. The world was fully good. It was in the beginning when God made heaven—and the earth. God made the world from nothing and gave it form. Turned on the lights. Hung the sky and made the seas. He made fruits and veggies and sun to grow them. When he was finished, the planet burst with fish and birds and animals. And the pinnacle of his creation—Adam and Eve, the first people—walked and talked with God in their own green paradise, the Garden of Eden. God surveyed all he had made and said, "Good stuff. Very good stuff." And earth was only a spit from heaven.

Then along came a snake in the grass.

God had given Adam and Eve one rule: Don't eat fruit from one special tree in the center of the garden. The snake in the grass—Satan, big time bad in a bod—asked Eve if she was sure about God's rule. Eve twisted God's words (she added another rule, that God told her not to *touch* the fruit). She distrusted God's goodness (she figured God wanted Adam and her stupid). Then she sinned openly. She disobeyed and ate. And Adam joined in.

You can get the great and gory details in Genesis 1–3, the first three chapters of the Bible. But here's the point: God and people no longer lived in harmony. The human race had joined Satan's war against God. Christians call what happened in the garden *The Fall*. It's not the best name. What Adam and Eve did was no slip—no *oops*. Maybe better to call it *The Leap to Evil*.

If you were God, what would you have done? You could have turned the planet into toast then and there. Or you could have forced people to obey you—upgraded their operating system, slicing out the code for disobedience and splicing in perfect Sunday school attendance, enthusiastic vegetable consumption, and quick and complete obedience to your commands.

Instead of toasting us, God let us freely go our own way. He let us keep our freedom to choose and to live as we pleased. The result? We wandered even farther from God. Apart from Christ, none of us understand him. None of us seek him. We have "together become corrupt; there is no one who does good, not even one" (Psalm 14:3). Our choice to sin has made a half-full/half-empty mess of the world.

Instead of toasting us, God worked to win us back. Our disobedience deserves death—not just an experience of our brains and bodies someday shutting down, but spiritual death: separation from God, starting now and lasting for eternity. God wouldn't stand for that. And his solution to our problem is familiar to Christians. He sent Jesus to die the death we deserved, so that those of us who believe in Jesus can live *together with him* for eternity. God "rescued us from the dominion of darkness and brought us into the kingdom of the Son he loves, in whom we have redemption, the forgiveness of sins" (Colossians 1:13–14).

Jesus' death and resurrection struck the winning blow

against evil. But Satan won't roll over and play dead. He's like a bad guy in a bad movie. He's in retreat. Wounded. Dripping blood. Reaching for his guns and still squeezing off rounds. And he's mad as hell.

The Heat is On

Some of us humans have settled with God. We have accepted God's offer of amnesty in Jesus—we've accepted God's forgiveness, laid down our weapons, quit the war. But some of us fight on.

Jesus said that at the end of time the battle between evil and good would heat up. Satan's side would rise up in one last fit of ugliness.

One day as Jesus and his followers were exiting the temple in Jerusalem, his guys were pointing out the sights like studly college dudes showing off their campus. Jesus wasn't impressed. He dropped a bomb—one day, he said, the temple would be destroyed. "Not one stone here will be left on another," he predicted.

Jesus' followers asked a pointed question.

> As Jesus was sitting on the Mount of Olives, the disciples came to him privately. "Tell us," they said, *"when will this happen, and what will be the sign of your coming and of the end of the age?"* (italics added)
>
> Matthew 24:3

Jesus gave a pointed answer. He saw way past the destruction of the temple—a catastrophic event that came to pass about forty years later—clear to the end of time. It's the Bible's most straightforward description of the end of everything, recorded for us to read in Matthew 24–25.

What Jesus said would happen first was a time of trials *before* the end—before a world-warping period of distress that would bring what we all think of as *the* end. There would be a time like "the beginning of birth pains," the uncomfortable contractions at the start of childbirth that signal the coming of even bigger agony. Listen to what Jesus said:

> Jesus answered: "Watch out that no one deceives you. For many will come in my name, claiming, 'I am the Christ,' and will deceive many. You will hear of wars and rumors of wars, but see to it that you are not alarmed. Such things must happen, but the end is still to come. Nation will rise against nation, and kingdom against kingdom. There will be famines and earthquakes in various places. All these are the beginning of birth pains.
>
> "Then you will be handed over to be persecuted and put to death, and you will be hated by all nations because of me. At that time many will turn away from the faith and will betray and hate each other, and many false prophets will appear and deceive many people. Because of the increase of wickedness, the love of most will grow cold, but he who stands firm to the end will be saved. And this gospel of the kingdom will be preached in the whole world as a testimony to all nations, and then the end will come" (italics added).
>
> Matthew 24:4–14

Jesus foresaw a mixture of bad and good in this "end before the end":

- *Political turbulence.* Wars and rumors of wars, nation rising against nation and kingdom against kingdom.
- *Natural disasters.* Famines and earthquakes.
- *Spiritual deception.* Falling away from the faith, increase in wickedness, loss of love for God, impostor "Christs," false prophets, and persecution.
- *Spiritual advance.* God's good news of Christ carried to all nations.

Three out of four of those categories are plenty scary. But Jesus made doubly clear they aren't the end of the world. "Such things must happen," he said, "but the end is still to come" (24:6). All these things will happen *before* the end comes (24:14).

Meanwhile—In Heaven

The chunk of human history Jesus described sounds a lot like a period detailed in the book of Revelation. Like this time of Birthpains it is a time *before* the end—prior to a time of unrestrained evil that ultimately brings the world to a crashing halt.

The first three chapters of Revelation are letters to seven churches in what is now western Turkey. The fourth and fifth chapters rocket to "what must take place after this," to a scene in heaven where Jesus—in all his resurrection splendor—is declared worthy to open the seals of a scroll that begin the events of the end. Chapter six starts with Christ breaking five seals. By the end of the chapter, breaking the sixth seal will start the "real" end of the world, a wild period when God pours his wrath on anyone who refuses to follow him.

With the breaking of each seal in heaven, something happens on earth. It's when the action heats up for us earthlings. Check out the similarities to what Jesus described in Matthew 24:

> I watched as the Lamb opened the first of the seven seals. Then I heard one of the four living creatures say in a voice like thunder, "Come!" I looked, and there before me was a white horse! Its rider held a bow, and he was given a crown, and he rode out as a conqueror bent on conquest.
> When the Lamb opened the second seal, I heard the second living creature say, "Come!" Then another horse

came out, a fiery red one. Its rider was given power to take peace from the earth and to make men slay each other. To him was given a large sword.

When the Lamb opened the third seal, I heard the third living creature say, "Come!" I looked, and there before me was a black horse! Its rider was holding a pair of scales in his hand. Then I heard what sounded like a voice among the four living creatures, saying, "A quart of wheat for a day's wages, and three quarts of barley for a day's wages, and do not damage the oil and the wine!"

When the Lamb opened the fourth seal, I heard the voice of the fourth living creature say, "Come!" I looked, and there before me was a pale horse! Its rider was named Death, and Hades was following close behind him. They were given power over a fourth of the earth to kill by sword, famine and plague, and by the wild beasts of the earth.

Revelation 6:1–8

Each time a seal on the scroll is broken, a horse and rider come forward. The identity of at least three horsemen are clear: The Second Horseman is *Bloodshed*. He rides a horse of fiery red, the color of slaughter. The Third Horseman is *Famine*. He ushers in a time when a whole day's pay would barely buy food—that quart of wheat could keep one person alive for a day, three quarts of barley a small family. The Fourth Horseman is *Death*. The First Horseman could be *Conquest*—a counterpart to bloodshed. If the horsemen do parallel what Jesus described in Matthew 24, then that somewhat puzzling white horse could be the preaching of God's Gospel to the world.

Are We at the Beginning of the End?

Lots of books written today declare that the human race is living on the edge of the end—fast approaching the end of *everything*—because our world looks like what Jesus described: a messy period of wars, famine, earthquakes, and persecution. But think about this: Jesus' disciples thought *they* were living in the time of Birthpains. They faced great upheaval—political turmoil, natural disasters, spiritual deception, and spiritual harvest. And the early church's belief that *they* were the generation facing the end pops up several times in Scripture. Check out what John wrote late in the first century, calling his day "the last hour": "Dear children, this is the last hour; and as you have heard that the antichrist is coming, even now many antichrists have come. This is how we know it is the last hour" (1 John 2:18).

The "last days" were back then? Aren't they now? Or are they in the way future?

Think about this: The clock has been ticking down toward the end since Christ's victory on the cross. We wait for the day of Christ's total reign, when "at the name of Jesus every knee should bow, in heaven and on earth and under the earth, and every tongue confess that Jesus Christ is Lord, to the glory of God the Father" (Philippians 2:10–11). The Birthpains—and probably the four horsemen of Revelation—mark the beginning of the end. They could be in the future near or far. But it's also possible that Jesus meant the Birthpains to describe the whole age from the start of the church until now. The Birthpains might be the jumbled period—bad and good all mixed together—that we call home.

Hang On Tight

Jesus made a big point of when this period would *end*—not of when it would *begin*. He offered two signs that will show without a doubt that the world is ready to explode, signs we haven't yet seen:

- A *Sign of Hope*. God's Good News will be preached to

all the peoples of the world—and then the end will come (Matthew 24:14). Something to ponder: Hundreds of missionary groups think the early years of the next decade could see the task of telling the world about Jesus finished. But "completing the task" can mean a variety of things, from starting churches among each people to actually preaching the gospel to every human alive. Time will tell.

- Jesus also told of a *Sign of Horror*. The signal that the next stage in the end of time has begun is the appearance of the "the abomination that causes desolation," or the man the Bible also calls the Antichrist (Matthew 24:15). More on this later.

The Great Wait . . . Before the Great Tribulation

Whoever lives during the Birthpains will face a period of waiting. Jesus' big point was, Don't panic! The end is coming . . . but not yet! "You will hear of wars and rumors of wars, but see to it that you are not alarmed. Such things must happen, but the end is still to come" (Matthew 24:6). These birth pain things are as much a sign that the end is *distant* as close by. It's a waiting game.

The wait is even clearer in Revelation. The first four seals bring the four galloping ghastlies. Then when the fifth seal is broken, believers who have been killed for their faith cry out: " 'How long, Sovereign Lord, holy and true, until you judge the inhabitants of the earth and avenge our blood?' " (Revelation 6:10). God's response? Wait a little longer. And a word even more unsettling: These martyrs were to wait until "the number of their fellow servants and brothers who were to be killed as they had been was completed" (Revelation 6:11).

"They're getting away with murder, God!" they protested. These followers of God had been good. But they'd been strung up by forces of evil. They'd paid the ultimate cost of obedience.

"Wait!" God says.

The war between good and evil rages on. God's judgment waits. But not for long. This half-full/half-empty world won't go on forever.

"There is no doubt that global events are preparing the way for the final war of history—the great Armageddon. As the earthly time clock ticks off each second and the world approaches midnight, this planet, according to the Bible, is going to be plunged into suffering too horrible to imagine or comprehend."

Billy Graham (b. 1918)
United States evangelist
Till Armageddon

5

The Grapes of Wrath

Jesus once told a story about a landowner who planted grapes. This landowner added everything his vineyard needed—a protective wall, a watchtower, a winepress—and rented his vineyard to some farmers. Then he left on a trip. When harvest time came he dispatched servants to collect rent—his share of the fruit. The farmers gladly paid up, right? Nope. They felt fortunate to care for such a fine bunch of vines, no doubt? Wrong. They beat the first servant. Bumped off the second. And bonked a third with rocks. Finally the landowner sent his son. The farmers murdered the son and tossed his body out of the vineyard.

Jesus turned and asked his hearers what the owner of the vineyard would do to those tenants. "He will bring those wretches," they snorted, "to a wretched end" (Matthew 21:41).

Wretching in the Vineyard

But those farmers aren't the only ones who need to fear the wrath of the Great Grape Landowner. From day one in the Garden of Eden, the human race has hung out—in *God's* garden—like a bunch of gun-toting, tequila-shooting, big hairy-bellied *banditos*. We've been on a spree of funky wine, tacky women, and out-of-tune song. We've lazed around doing our own thing, peeking out over the walls only to take pot shots at God. We chased off his servants. We killed his son. We refused his offer of a truce.

Two thousand years later a lot of us haven't put down our weapons.

A wretched end awaits any who refuse God's mercy.

God's offer of a truce still stands. He's patient, waiting for us to accept the forgiveness he provides in Christ. He'd rather see us surrender to him than keep fighting for the losing side—you won't believe how sore the losers of this war against God will be.

A wretched end awaits any who refuse God's mercy.

God realizes, though, that his long wait for humankind to halt its rebellion won't solve the sin problem. Sin has squished out all over. God has squashed back with the Gospel. Yet the Bible foresees a time when evil will strengthen in an all-out, end-of-time push of disobedience.

In fact, as bad as the Birthpains are, the battle between good and evil gets worse. Jesus summed up what this next stage would look like: "For then there will be *great distress*, unequaled from the beginning of the world until now—and never to be equaled again" (italics added; Matthew 24:21). Great . . . distress . . . unequaled . . . never. It's world-whomping stuff:

It's the ultimate trial, the *Tribulation*—what the New International Version of the Bible calls a *Great Distress*.

It's the time of the *Beast*—the *Antichrist*—the *666* guy.

It's the forerunner of *Armageddon*—earth's final battle.

It's the last thing before the *Apocalypse*—the second appearing of Jesus Christ—the high point of cosmic history for those who love God, doomsday for those who don't. *A wretched end awaits any who refuse God's mercy.*

The Rise of the Ultimate Stupid Guy

Get it straight up front: This is earth's ugliest hour. And there's a reason life gets so distressing. In the time of Great Distress people not only follow false Christs (Matthew 24:23–26), they chase *the* false Christ. They fall for the ultimate alternative to God: the Antichrist.

Surprise: The term "Antichrist" appears nowhere in Revelation. But this shadowy figure pops up several times in Scripture. He's like an evil action figure on after-school TV. He looks foreboding enough at the start—but when you look at all the descriptions of him in Scripture, he morphs into utterly monstrous evil:

- *He's the signal at the start of the Great Distress.* "So when you see standing in the holy place 'the abomination that causes desolation,' spoken of through the prophet Daniel . . ." (Matthew 24:15). Daniel foresaw a ruler who will make a seven-year peace treaty with the nation of Israel, then break it after three and a half years, touching off the nastiest period of evil. The "abomination of desolation" is his setting up an idol— himself, or an image of himself—in the temple (Daniel 9:27; 11:31; 12:11).

- *He's the "man of lawlessness"* who arrives on the scene prior to Christ's second coming. Paul writes, "Concerning the coming of our Lord Jesus Christ and our being gathered to him . . . that day will not come until the rebellion occurs and the man of lawlessness is revealed, the man doomed to destruction. He opposes and exalts himself over everything that is called God or is worshiped, and even sets himself up in God's temple, proclaiming himself to be God" (2 Thessalonians 2:1, 3–4). The man of lawlessness is tricky: His coming will be "in accordance with the work of Satan displayed in all kinds of counterfeit miracles, signs and wonders, and in every sort of evil that deceives those who are perishing" (2 Thessalonians 2:9–10).

- *He's the Antichrist in John's first and second letters*, the worst of a whole assortment of impostors. "Dear children, this is the last hour; and as you have heard that the antichrist is coming, even now many antichrists have come. This is how we know it is the last hour" (1 John 2:18). Antichrists are those who deny that Jesus is the Savior of the world (1 John 2:22).

- *He's the beast of Revelation.* He arises from the sea— probably meaning from non-Jewish peoples—at the will of "the Dragon," Satan himself (13:1). He is fatally wounded—but when he recovers all the world worships him (13:3).

The Beast Onstage

Revelation tells us plenty more about this Beast. He looks bizarre when he struts on stage. He's got ten horns topped with ten crowns—and that's besides seven heads, on each head a name vicious toward God (13:2). How he looks symbolizes his raw ability to do evil—horns in Scripture stand for strength (Christ, for example, has seven horns in Revelation 5:6), and crowns for power and leadership (again, you can spot a good crown in Revelation 14:14). Many writers today interpret this symbolism to mean the Antichrist will rule a ten-nation bloc from Rome or the Middle East.

More significant than how the Antichrist looks, though, is what he does. He openly defies God. He demands worship from all. And he offers the planet a choice: Deny Christ or die. Humankind has gotten used to following false gods—all the things they make so important they become substitutes for the one true God—so that all but those who know Jesus save their skins by obeying the Beast: "All inhabitants of the earth will worship the beast—all whose name have not been written in the book of life belonging to the Lamb that was slain from the creation of the world" (Revelation 13:8).

The Beast is best known for his 666 brand: "He also forced everyone, small and great, rich and poor, free and slave, to receive a mark on his right hand or on his forehead, so that no one could buy or sell unless he had the mark, which is the name of the beast or the number of his name . . . 666" (Revelation 13:16–18). Exactly what the "mark of the beast" is isn't clear. Christians—the ones whose names are written in the book of life—get their own forehead stamp, a sign of God's protection (Revelation 7:3; 9:4). Whatever these marks are—whether they are even physical or not—they are a sign of submission. God's mark says God owns your heart. The Beast's mark says you belong to him.

So picture this: Without the mark you'd be shut out of the Gap and Goodwill, Burger King and Taco Bell—and every other shop-until-you-drop and scarf-until-you-barf establishment. It'd be like losing your locker combination, forgetting your class schedule, and permanently *whoops*-ing down a sewer your cash, plastic, ATM card, checkbook, and driver's license. You wouldn't exist.

The Untrusty Sidekick

The Beast doesn't act alone. He has a sidekick, the "False Prophet" (Revelation 16:13). Just as the Beast wields ungodly political and economic power, the false prophet helps rule the world through fake religion. The Beast is a dictator. The false prophet is more of a sorcerer, the high priest of a one-world religion.

The false prophet appears as an imitator of Christ—with "two horns like a lamb"—but he speaks like Satan (Revelation 13:11). He has a bag of big tricks, including the ability to cause fire to fall from heaven (Revelation 13:13). And he tops off his act with a you-can't-miss-it miraculous sign. He makes an image of the Beast live: "He deceived the inhabitants of the earth. He ordered them to set up an image in honor of the beast. . . . He was given power to give breath to the image of the first beast, so that it could speak and cause all who refused to worship the image to be killed" (Revelation 13:14–15). The false prophet makes all the earth bow before the Beast—or be bonked. Together the Antichrist and false prophet rule a political-economic-religious order dead set against God.

Take a Breather

No doubt about it: This is Scripture's scariest stuff. It's probably *meant* to be. It shows all Christians the do-or-die seriousness of making the right choice: Jesus. Moreover, Revelation was a real book written to real people facing real death for refusing to worship Domitian, the emperor of Rome from A.D. 81 to 96. Those suffering Christians surely found hope in the book's big points: *Worship only God* (14:11), *hang tight to Jesus* (14:12), *endure persecution patiently* (12:17; 13:7), and *God will one day zing you home to heaven* (7:13–17). It's a heavy message—but straight talk for a world where following Jesus is a live-or-die choice. Sadly, it's also a timely message today—because even right now *many* Christians around the world face harassment, beatings, imprisonment, and death for their faith.

But God doesn't want you worried for the wrong reasons or running scared of the wrong person. People have played "pin the tail on the Antichrist" for 2,000 years. They've guessed that the Beast is everyone from the Roman emperor Nero to Saddam Hussein, Kaiser Wilhelm, Adolf Hitler, Benito Mussolini, Henry Kissinger, any number of popes, Mikhail Gorbachev, Ronald Wilson Reagan (six letters in each name—must be that bad ol' 666), and Bill Clinton (accompanied by—take your pick—"false prophetess" Hillary or "eco-priest" Al Gore).

Take off the blindfold and look at these facts: *No one will take the mark of the beast by accident.* The mark is a sign of a deliberate choice to worship a world leader other than God, to offer your life and allegiance to a religious, economic, and political system other than Jesus (Revelation 16:2). Clear on that? You don't get the mark by letting the quickmart guy scan the bar code on your Twinkies. Or by using an ATM machine or a debit card. Or by getting tattooed or silicon-chipped in your sleep. More than that, *no one who truly loves God will be mistaken about what the mark means.* Remember? By this point in future human history God's Good News about Jesus has been preached to the whole planet. The world is clear on who God is (Matthew 24:14). The Beast openly defies the one true God, and those who take the mark openly chuck that real God and obey the Beast instead. And check out Revelation 14:6–11 for what seems to be God's clear, final, supernatural warning.

God Strikes Back

During the Great Distress the Antichrist rampages against anyone who follows God. But a second factor makes the Great Distress so greatly distressing: God punishes everyone who chooses to follow anyone but him.

A world of sin isn't what God had planned. He won't allow this half-full/half-empty world to go on forever. Evil has refused to go down without a fight. And so humanity's ultimate rebellion brings God's ultimate response.

God is mad. But he doesn't use force without reason. He isn't a kid who heads for a sidewalk with a magnifying glass to fry bugs in the sun. He doesn't tie dragonflies on leashes or pull legs from spiders. He's like a teacher busting a fight. Or a SWAT team swooping and shooting to the rescue. Or a massed military force shutting down wrongful aggression.

So why is God so mad? What finally makes him act? Why the Great Distress?

His wisdom knows it's time to *expose evil*.

His righteousness compels him to *punish evil*.

His compassion moves him to *destroy evil*.

The apostle Paul wrote that "in the last days" people will ditch God and everything good. They'll be "lovers of themselves, lovers of money, boastful, proud, abusive, disobedient to their parents, ungrateful, unholy, without love, unforgiving, slanderous, without self-control, brutal, not lovers of the good, treacherous, rash, conceited, lovers of pleasure rather than lovers of God—having a form of godliness but denying its power" (2 Timothy 3:2–5).

Revelation makes the same point. Even after God begins to pour out punishment people "still did not repent of the work of their hands; they did not stop worshiping demons, and idols of gold, silver, bronze, stone and wood—idols that cannot see or hear or walk. Nor did they repent of their murders, their magic arts, their sexual immorality or their thefts. . . . They were seared by the intense heat and they cursed the name of God, who had control over these plagues, but they refused to repent and glorify him" (Revelation 9:20–21; 16:9). At the end of time, people disobey God worse than ever. They disbelieve his love. They distrust the rules his kindness designed. Human rebellion is alive and kicking hard. So God grabs evil like a cowboy grabs a bull by the horns. This bull, though, won't be tossing the cowboy up in the air, flinging him to the ground, or stomping on his chest. This bull is going down. There will come a day when God says, "TIME IS UP! ENOUGH CHANCES! EVIL WILL STOP!"

God's end-of-time punishment of the world's sin starts in earnest with Revelation 6:13. This is where you need to put on your thinking cap. Imagine *end of evil*. Ponder *death of bad*. Expect *display of God's power*. Snap on the chin strap and hang on tight—this gets wild.

The first four seals of Revelation 6 loosed "the four horsemen of the apocalypse," and the fifth seal showed God's people crying out for revenge on evildoers. Here's what the sixth seal brings:

> I watched as he opened the sixth seal. There was a great earthquake. The sun turned black like sackcloth made of goat hair, the whole moon turned blood red, and the stars in the sky fell to earth, as late figs drop from a fig tree when shaken by a strong wind. The sky receded like a scroll, rolling up, and every mountain and island was removed from its place.
>
> Then the kings of the earth, the princes, the generals, the rich, the mighty, and every slave and every free man hid in caves and among the rocks of the mountains. They called to the mountains and the rocks, "Fall on us and hide us from the face of him who sits on the throne and from the wrath of the Lamb! For the great day of their wrath has come, and who can stand?"
>
> Revelation 6:12–17

It's the beginning of God's wrath. The sky retracts like a scroll—like a spring-loaded tape measure, *kazshinnnng SNAP!*—and the world reacts with a swirl of blood, tears, and nervous sweat.

The Seventh Seal and Seven Trumpets

The seventh seal is when the action really gets hot. When that seal is opened, there is silence in heaven, then seven angels are given seven trumpets to sound (Revelation 8:1–2). As with the seals, each time something happens in heaven, a corresponding something takes place on earth. As each trumpet sounds in heaven, disaster strikes earth. Stand back and watch a quick catalog of what awaits those who do evil:

- *The First Trumpet.* Hail and fire mixed with blood are hurled at earth. A third of the earth, a third of the trees, and all the green grass burn up (8:7).
- *The Second Trumpet.* Something like a huge burning mountain is thrown into the sea. A third of the sea turns into blood, a third of the living creatures in the sea die, and a third of the ships are destroyed (8:8).
- *The Third Trumpet.* A great star falls from the sky on a third of the rivers and springs. A third of the waters turn bitter. Many people die from the fouled waters (8:10–11).
- *The Fourth Trumpet.* A third of the sun, moon, and stars are struck. A third of the day is without light, and also a third of the night (8:12).
- *The Fifth Trumpet.* Locusts come out from the Abyss, the home of demons. They have the sting of scorpions, and power to torture for five months all who do not have the seal of God on their foreheads. *Sooo* bad: "During those days men will seek death, but will not find it; they will long to die, but death will elude them" (9:1–6).
- *The Sixth Trumpet.* Four angels—fallen, demonic angels—are released to kill a third of humankind. An army of two hundred million troops kill a third of all earthlings (9:13–16).

The Seven Bowls

The seventh seal unwrapped seven trumpets. But there's more. Now the seventh trumpet begins a pouring out of seven bowls of God's wrath. These bowls mark the end of God's punishment of the planet: "I saw in heaven another great and marvelous sign: seven angels with the seven last plagues—*last, because with them God's wrath is completed.* . . . Then one of the four living creatures gave to the seven angels seven golden bowls filled with the wrath of God, who lives for ever and ever" (italics added; Revelation 15:1, 7).

There's nothing sugar-coated about the stuff in these bowls. Sinners choke on a most unappetizing breakfast:

- *The First Bowl.* Ugly and painful sores break out on the people who have the mark of the beast and worship his image (16:2).
- *The Second Bowl.* The sea turns into blood "like that of a dead man," and everything in the sea dies (16:3).
- *The Third Bowl.* Rivers and springs become blood (16:4).
- *The Fourth Bowl.* The sun scorches people with intense fire (16:8).
- *The Fifth Bowl.* The kingdom of the Beast is plunged into darkness and men gnaw their tongues in agony (16:10).
- *The Sixth Bowl.* The waters of the Euphrates River dry up to prepare the way for an invasion by "the kings from the East." Three demons that look like frogs come out of the mouths of the dragon, Beast, and false prophet. They gather the kings to battle God at a place called Armageddon (16:12–13, 16).
- *The Seventh Bowl.* A loud voice comes from the throne, saying, "It is done!" And then comes lightning, thunder, and the biggest earthquake of all time (16:17–18).

With that seventh bowl God shouts, "It's done!"

Exactly *what* is done?

Read on. In the next couple chapters you'll see exactly how the Great Distress ends. Here's a hint: God wins. And so does everybody on his side.

He who testifies to
these things says,
"Yes, I am coming soon."
Amen.
Come, Lord Jesus.

John the Apostle
Revelation 22:20

6

All Hail King Jesus

Put yourself in God's size *infinite* shoes for a second.

If God had a bod, he'd be beyond huge. His shoe would slap down over a dozen galaxies—no, it's more like a mole on his baby toe would dwarf the universe. Slow down and read that again. *Hmmm . . . size of baby toe mole vs. size of universe.* Got it? And even that comparison doesn't bring it into proportion. All the distances your mind can begin to imagine would be less than the breadth of one of God's hairs.

Now, make no mistake: God doesn't have a body. But contemplate the hugeness of his goodness, brains, and might. He is Infinite Love, Infinite Knowledge, Infinite Power.

Along comes humankind trying to pick a fight—thinking that we're kinder, smarter, and stronger than God. Next to him we're a bunch of unibrows—a horde of tiny, sloped-foreheaded cavemen banging clubs on his toes. *Duh.* We're creatures rising up against the Creator. *Dumb.*

We have no idea what we're up against.

We're way less than God. Sin has made us a bunch of back-of-the-classroom dunces. Always-picked-last-for-the-team losers. Leave-her-picture-out-of-the-yearbook uglies. Here's the shocker: God still has chosen us for friendship with himself. He made us capable of knowing him. He bequeathed us with the dignity of being able to freely choose for or against him. He loved us before we ever showed any love toward him. And he's coming back for those of us who belong to him. It's the next step after the Great Distress:

> Immediately after the distress of those days "the sun will be darkened, and the moon will not give its light; the stars will fall from the sky, and the heavenly bodies will be shaken." At that time the sign of the Son of Man will appear in the sky, and all the nations of the earth will mourn. They will see the Son of Man coming on the clouds of the sky, with power and great glory. And he will send his angels with a loud trumpet call, and they will gather his elect from the four winds, from one end of the heavens to the other.
>
> Matthew 24:29–31

The skies will jump. The world will mourn. Jesus will rescue his people ("his elect") and reign over all.

Jesus is coming back. It's the heart of the Bible's message about the end of the world: Jesus "loves us and has freed us from our sins by his blood. . . . Look, he is coming with the clouds" (Revelation 1:5–7).

Jesus is the big deal. His return is the kingly victory Scripture prophesied way back when. Even before Jesus came the first time, Daniel wrote about what Jesus' second appearing would look like: "In my vision at night I looked, and there before me was one like a son of man, coming with the clouds of heaven. He approached the Ancient of Days and was led into his presence. He was given authority, glory and sovereign power; all peoples, nations and men of every language worshiped him. His dominion is an everlasting dominion that will not pass away, and his kingdom is one that will never be destroyed" (Daniel 7:13–14).

Back Up a Bit

Flashback. The Birthpains will end with a Sign of Hope: God's Good News preached "in the whole world as a testimony to all nations, and then the end will come" (Matthew 24:14)—and with a Sign of Horror: the "abomination that causes desolation" standing in "the holy place" (Matthew 24:15). Those events signal the beginning of the Great Distress, the age of the Antichrist.

That suffering spell will swallow the whole planet—it "will come upon all those who live on the face of the whole earth" (Luke 21:35). And it will last for a stretch of predetermined time, according to a timetable set by God.

Many writers feel the Bible reveals the exact duration of the Distress. In a chunk of time Daniel calls "the seventieth week" they see a tribulation lasting seven years (Daniel 9:24–27). The second half of these seven years—often called the "Great Tribulation"—is seen as the most intense period of evil ugliness. It's measured in a variety of ways: three and a half years (Daniel 9:27), forty-two months (Revelation 11:2), 1,260 days (Revelation 11:3), or "a time, and times, and half a time" (Revelation 12:14).

Jesus puts all of our estimating in perspective. He says that if God didn't call a halt to those days *no one* would survive—and that the period of Distress has indeed been cut short "for the sake of the elect" (Matthew 24:22). Besides that, the main points of this last flare-up in the war between good and bad are clear. *The Great Distress is a period of unbelievable evil.* Satan and the Beast lead the world in rebellion and in persecution of believers. *The Great Distress is an outpouring of God's wrath.* God punishes those who refuse to repent and surrender to him. And like the times before it, *the Great Distress will come to an end.*

Back to the Show

We may be fuzzy about the timing of the Birthpains. We may even wonder a bit about the beginning of the Tribulation—the Great Distress. But there won't be any mistaking the arrival of Jesus.

When Jesus left earth after his crucifixion and resurrection, he made his exit from the Mount of Olives, outside Jerusalem. As Jesus spoke to his disciples "he was taken up before their very eyes, and a cloud hid him from their sight" (Acts 1:9). The disciples were gawking at the sky when two angels suddenly appeared to them. " 'Men of Galilee,' they said, 'why do you stand here looking into the sky? This same Jesus, who has been taken from you into heaven, will come back in the same way you have seen him go into heaven' " (Acts 1:11).

No one will miss the sky-filling fireworks. Jesus is coming back in the same way he left. On the clouds. And with the sky shaking. The sun and moon darkened. Stars falling from the sky. Jesus summed it up: "For as the lightning comes from the east and flashes to the west, so will be the coming of the Son of Man" (Matthew 24:27).

And no one will miss what Jesus' entrance means. Remember? With the seventh bowl, God booms from his throne, "It is done!" (Revelation 16:17). When Jesus arrives, *it means God's perfect kingdom is here.*

So What's Done?

God has always been in charge. But at the end of time he takes the authority that is rightfully his and asserts his reign. Revelation 11 foreshadows what the arrival of Christ's kingdom will look like:

"The kingdom of the world has become the kingdom of our Lord and of his Christ, and he will reign for ever and ever." And the twenty-four elders, who were seated on their thrones before God, fell on their faces and worshiped God, saying: "We give thanks to you, Lord God Almighty, who is and who was, because you have taken your great power and have begun to reign. The nations were angry; and your wrath has come. The time has come for judging the dead, and for rewarding your servants the prophets and your saints and those who reverence your name, both small and great—and for destroying those who destroy the earth."

Revelation 11:15–18

Arrival. Reign. Judgment. Reward. And it's all executed through the exalted Christ: "God exalted him [Jesus] to the highest place and gave him the name that is above every name, that at the name of Jesus every knee should bow, in heaven and on earth and under the earth, and every tongue confess that Jesus Christ is Lord, to the glory of God the Father" (Philippians 2:9–11). At the end of time *everyone* will admit Jesus is Lord of the Universe. Everyone—angels in heaven, people on earth, Satan and his sidekicks in hell—will bow willingly to Jesus. Or be bent by God.

"It is done!" means God has brought to completion the perfect kingdom he planned since before the beginning of the world. "It is done!" means all of his plans are accomplished. Jesus arrives and mops up the last of evil. (More on that in the next chapter, "Liar, Liar, Pants on Fire.") Jesus arrives and pulls his people to himself. (More on that in chapter 8, "Where Are We Through All of This?") And Jesus arrives and jump starts eternity. That's when the fun begins.

Let the Good Times Roll

In God's scheme of things his wrath is relatively insignificant. It's a blip. A speed bump. A booger to be blown out

It's No Fairytale

Here's why heaven is so great. It ain't home to princely hunks or fairy princesses. The magic kingdom is real. God's people live happily ever after. It's a paradisal place. It's re-made people. It's living in the *light* of the party, God himself.

God's rule would be no good if he were a lousy king. Jesus obviously has the *might* to rule us. He has the raw power to force our respect, to put us in a headlock until our brains break. There's more to his rule than that. Jesus also has the *right* to rule us.

It's easy to imagine a universe ruled by a monster. Where the guy with the baddest belch wins. Where a King Kong battles a Godzilla. Where one of the brutes happens to beat the other and become king over all—but he's still a monster.

Jesus doesn't just muscle our obedience. His total goodness commands our respect. He's what the Bible calls "worthy." He's worthy of our praise because he saves us from our enemies (2 Samuel 22:4). Because he is to be "feared above all gods" (1 Chronicles 16:25). Because his greatness is beyond imagination (Psalm 145:3). In Revelation, the twenty-four elders surround the throne of God to shout "You are worthy, our Lord and God, to receive glory and honor and power, for you created all things, and by your will they were created and have their being" (Revelation 4:11). Jesus is worthy of *glory*—wearing the shining majesty of God's presence. *Honor*—receiving respect that reaches to the stars. And *power*—wielding unlimited might and authority.

We can't give him those things. He already has them as unfailing parts of his being. But we can recognize them. We shout to Jesus, "YOU THE MAN!" Except it's "YOU THE GOD OF ALL!"

Jesus is the one being capable of running the universe. Satan offers dictatorship. Jesus offers Lordship. We submit to him gladly. Dictators seize control. God invites us to give ourselves willingly.

He's the right God for the job. He's the one real God. He's the only one capable of running the planet. He's the only one fit to look after our lives. Life with him—friendship with the worthy one—is the only thing that can satisfy us.

Christians trust that. They welcome the coming of the kingdom of God in the person of Jesus. They look forward to heaven, his hoppin' place.

Not everyone does.

When Jesus comes he ushers in heaven. But he has another job. He comes to smash evil.

"There are two equal and opposite errors into which our race can fall about the devils. One is to disbelieve in their existence. The other is to believe, and to feel an excessive and unhealthy interest in them. They themselves are equally pleased by both errors...."

C. S. Lewis (1898-1963)
British author
The Screwtape Letters

7

Liar, Liar, Pants on Fire

Sulfur boils at 832.3 degrees Fahrenheit.

Hot enough for you?

To say the eulogy at Satan's funeral would be pretty simple: See Satan. Satan sins. Satan leads human race in rebellion. See Jesus trounce Satan on the cross. See Satan struggle to stay in charge of planet earth. See Jesus toss Satan into lake of burning sulfur. See Satan *a-bubba-bubblin'*. Forever. Amen.

From way back Satan has headed an alternative kingdom. Led every charge in the war against God. Been living proof that lots of times Bad Guys Finish First.

But fast-forward to the end of time: Jesus comes back. He ushers in heaven. He undoes evil. Ha! *Look who's toast now!*

Never Born to Be Wild

A few chapters back we saw Satan as a snake in the Garden of Eden. While that's his first appearance in the Bible—about page 3 or so—it isn't *chronologically* the beginning of the Satan story. The Bible hints at Satan's beginning as a high angel—maybe even the peak of God's creation. Back before he became His Royal Ugliness, he was "the model of perfection, full of wisdom and perfect in beauty . . . every precious stone adorned you: ruby, topaz and emerald, chrysolite, onyx and jasper, sapphire, turquoise and beryl." He was stunning—as if he were studded with jewels—and a studly "guardian cherub" (Ezekiel 28:12–14).

Not all cherubs (or "cherubim") are chubby little guys content to shoot arrows on Valentine's Day. Satan was beefy. And he got stuck on his own incredible beauty (1 Timothy 3:6). Isaiah fills in the story of how Satan tried to take God's place as ruler of the universe: "How you have fallen from heaven, O morning star, son of the dawn! . . . You said in your heart, 'I will ascend to heaven; I will raise my throne above the stars of God; I will sit enthroned on the mount of assembly, on the utmost heights of the sacred mountain. . . . I will make myself like the Most High' " (Isaiah 14:12–14).

His actions since that first rebellion add up to a long rap sheet:

Satan is a rebel and he'll never be any good. The devil has always looked for a way around God's rules. And he's always looked for partners in his crimes against the Creator. He tempted Adam and Eve (Genesis 3:1–24). He even tempted Jesus (Matthew 4:1–11). He's "the spirit who is now at work in those who are disobedient" (Ephesians 2:2).

We can't blame Satan totally for our being tempted—the Bible, in fact, says we are drawn away from doing right by our own wrong desires (James 1:13–15). We can't blame Satan when we blow it—the Bible also says God won't allow us to be tempted beyond what we can handle (1 Corinthians 10:13). Even so, we can resist Satan and make him run from us (James 4:7).

Satan is our adversary. He's no Darth Vadar—a make-believe King-of-the-Evildoers. He doesn't put on a dark helmet, wheeze hard and deep, and say, "You, come over to the dark side." He's slyer than that. And he's no deviant-but-basically-harmless child brat—a Macaulay-Culkin-doing-*Home-Alone* look-alike. Left on his own, Satan would be the undoing of the universe. He and his gang can cause real pain: things like illness (Luke 13:16) and demonic "possession" or "demonization" (Luke 22:3). He's the prince of the planet and the whole world is in his grip (1 John 5:19). We struggle against "the powers of this dark world and against the spiritual forces of evil in the heavenly realms" (Ephesians 6:12). This is one enemy God doesn't require you to love.

Satan is our accuser. Christians mess up. Plenty. God promises, though, that if we admit our sins he will forgive us and make us clean again (1 John 1:8–9). He gives our relationship a fresh start each and every time.

Even though Jesus has made us once-and-for-all right with God—and even though confessing sin and trusting God's forgiveness lets us enjoy God's gracious friendship—Satan wants us to still feel guilty. To act like we have something to hide. To avoid God's eyes and run away when we hear him coming. Satan retains enough authority on earth and status in heaven to go before God and shriek that we are still guilty. His accusations ring in our ears back on earth. Want to plug your ears? Cling to God's promises of forgiveness through Christ's shed blood (Revelation 12:10–11).

Satan is a liar. The root of Satan's tempting, torturing, and accusing is *the* lie: He says that "God isn't good." From that lie flows every other lie: "God doesn't deserve to be God." "Satan would be a better god." "We can be the god of our own lives."

Satan's twisted tongue is so much a part of who he is

and how he acts in the world that Jesus called him "a liar and the father of lies" (John 8:44).

Beating Back the Bully

Satan is the ultimate liar. And one day his pants will be on fire.

Little by little, Satan's rebellion is being beaten back. When the disciples went out and witnessed that in Jesus the kingdom of God had arrived, Satan fell like lightning from heaven (Luke 10:18). When Jesus died and rose he took away Satan's power to hold us hostage through sin and death. He "disarmed the powers and authorities" and "made a public spectacle of them, triumphing over them by the cross" (Colossians 2:15). And whenever one of us stops rebelling against God, Satan's army has one less soldier. Jesus has "rescued us from the dominion of darkness and brought us into the kingdom of the Son he loves, in whom we have redemption, the forgiveness of sins" (Colossians 1:13–14).

At the end of time Satan will at last be completely excluded from heaven. "He [he's called the Dragon in this passage] was hurled to the earth, and his angels with him" (Revelation 12:9). No one deserves to be hurled more than Satan. It's when he gets really hot—he knows his time is almost up (Revelation 12:12).

That's where we get back into the plot line of the last few chapters. Satan's hurling is probably the time he kicks off the Great Distress, raising up the Antichrist in his final attempt to deceive and destroy God's people. He establishes his all-powerful economic, political, and religious system through the Beast. Then somewhere in this time frame God strikes back at evil, first with the disasters announced by the seven trumpets, then with the plagues poured from the bowls of God's wrath.

Hailing on the Rebel Horde

If the sixth bowl is like the pre-game show for the end, then the seventh bowl is the kickoff. We already saw that with the sixth bowl demons go gather "kings from the east" to Armageddon. With the seventh bowl God shouts, "It is done!" In the last chapter we saw how at God's "It is done!" Jesus ushered in heaven. Now we'll see how he mops up evil.

He starts with a hailstorm. The sky heaves ice rocks "of about a hundred pounds each" (Revelation 16:21). That's worse than getting doinked on the head by a golf ball—it's more like six bowling balls lashed together with duct tape.

The exact meaning of "Armageddon" isn't clear. The name could be from the Hebrew name *Har Megeddon,* "the mountain of Megiddo." But that's a pretty small spot to the northwest of Jerusalem—a bit like saying this Ultimate Super Bowl is going to be played in your bedroom, fans and all. Armageddon could simply be a shorthand name for God's final overthrow of evil, rather than a geographical clue.

That's the tail end of Revelation 16. In chapters 17 and 18 the Beast turns against what is called "Babylon" or "the great prostitute" or "the whore of Babylon." The powers that pulled together the Antichrist's false worldwide political, economic, and religious entities begin to destroy one another—and with that infighting, the one-world system collapses.

Not a Fair Fight

It's in chapter 19 that Satan meets his match. Only Satan's no match at all for Jesus, who rides in on a white stallion to bash evil. His entrance is too suave not to read about firsthand:

> I saw heaven standing open and there before me was

a white horse, whose rider is called Faithful and True. With justice he judges and makes war. His eyes are like blazing fire, and on his head are many crowns. He has a name written on him that no one but he himself knows. He is dressed in a robe dipped in blood, and his name is the Word of God. The armies of heaven were following him, riding on white horses and dressed in fine linen, white and clean. Out of his mouth comes a sharp sword with which to strike down the nations. "He will rule them with an iron scepter." He treads the winepress of the fury of the wrath of God Almighty. On his robe and on his thigh he has this name written: KING OF KINGS AND LORD OF LORDS.

Revelation 19:11–16

It's more than a tad dramatic. Jesus rides into battle flanked by the armies of heaven—apparently a host of angels. God's forces don't even need to join in. Jesus' weapon of choice is no thermonuclear warhead or neutron bomb. Not even his pinky. He strikes down the nations with his word, that sharp sword that comes out of his mouth.

The Beast and the false prophet thought they could fight God. Jesus merely speaks and they go up in smoke.

The Demise of Satan

These last few scenes from the end of time are the world's biggest barbecue. (Can't you see it? God thundering from his throne, "Toss another devil on the barby, mate.") Revelation tells us that the Beast and the false prophet are "thrown alive into the fiery lake of burning sulfur." The kings and armies that accompany them are killed by Christ's word, "and all the birds gorged themselves," eating "the flesh of kings, generals, and mighty men, of horses and their riders, and the flesh of all people, free and slave, great and small" (19:17–21).

Burp.

The battle of Armageddon spells doom for Satan as well. But he meets a different fate—for a little while, at least. An angel swoops out of heaven, picks him up, binds him with chains, and drops him in a place called "the Abyss" for a thousand years. The angel drops the lid and double locks it (Revelation 20:1–3). The Abyss is the ugly place the Beast came from (Revelation 11:7), and its name means "bottomless." Can't be a happy time for the Big Bad Guy.

Double burp.

Christians have argued about the meaning of the next few verses of Revelation for a couple thousand years—oddly enough, twice as long as Satan will be locked up, because the point of Revelation 20:1–10 is that Satan is bound for a thousand years and then loosed, allowed one more shot at deceiving the earth.

People who call themselves *pre*millennialists believe that these thousand years—the "millennium"—will be a special time of Christ reigning on earth along with believers. In their view, Christ will return to earth *after* all the nasty stuff described in Revelation, but *before* the millennium. *Post*millennialists believe Christ will return and reign forever *after* the millennium—in other words, life in the world gets *better* before Christ comes back. And people called *a*millennialists believe the thousand years described here aren't a literal thousand years—the "a" in "amillennialist" means "no." Some amillennialists think this passage describes believers who have died and are reigning with Christ in heaven right now. As radically different as these views are, strong Christians have held to each.

No one disagrees, though, on Satan's final demise. Revelation 20:10 puts it simply: "And the devil, who deceived them, was thrown into the lake of burning sulfur, where the beast and the false prophet had been thrown. They will be

tormented day and night for ever and ever."
Triple burp.

Get a Clue

Time out. Wrap together all that you've read about God's wrath against sin. You'd be warped not to get the message: God takes rebellion very seriously.

We all agree that Satan deserves every lick he gets—his thousand-year tumble into the bottomless pit, not to mention an eternity in a hot sulfur stew that reeks of rotten eggs. We even all agree that really bad people should get their due. No one winces when a Timothy McVeigh gets thrown in the jug. And not many protest when a jury decides to go for the jugular.

Here's the way harder part to hear: The whole human race is under God's judgment. We all answer to him.

Strange. We think we can beat the system. Deke God. Outwit omniscience.

It's like this. Suppose that fifteen minutes before the end of class, your social studies teacher heads to the school office, leaving you and a roomful of fellow inmates alone. Listen to the logic that bangs through the brain of any student who's breathing:

1. *Teacher probably isn't coming back before the bell.*

2. *I can goof off and teacher won't catch me.*

3. *Even if teacher does come back and does find me goofing off, he won't do anything about it.*

4. *Even if teacher decides to punish me, I can talk my way out of it.*

5. And *even if I can't talk my way out of the punishment, the fun I'll have is worth whatever short-term pain he inflicts.*

Reasonable enough. You may be able to dupe your teacher. You may be able to ward off detention. But Jesus is way smarter than your teacher. And the consequences are way bigger than sitting for an hour writing "I won't be evil ever again." Better chew on these reality bites:

- *You can count on Christ's return.* " 'Behold, I am coming soon! My reward is with me, and I will give to everyone according to what he has done' " (Revelation 22:12).
- *You can't hide sin.* "O LORD, you have searched me and you know me. You know when I sit and when I rise; you perceive my thoughts from afar. You discern my going out and my lying down; you are familiar with all my ways" (Psalm 139:1–3).
- *You can't escape judgment.* "Man is destined to die once, and after that to face judgment" (Hebrews 9:27).
- *You can't talk your way out of punishment.* "Since you call on a Father who judges each man's work impartially, live your lives as strangers here in reverent fear" (1 Peter 1:17). That's addressed to Christians.
- *You won't enjoy the punishment.* "If anyone's name was not found written in the book of life, he was thrown into the lake of fire" (Revelation 20:15). Hell isn't like a bad summer camp where you look around and squirm—but after a few days decide you can get used to it.

Jesus said that at the end of time he will sort between "sheep" and "goats," those who know him and those who don't (Matthew 25:31–46). John wrote that we would face a judgment before "a great white throne" (Revelation 20:11–15).

Paul's second letter to the Thessalonians makes clearer what all this means, in maybe the plainest warning in the whole Bible: "This will happen when the Lord Jesus is revealed from heaven in blazing fire with his powerful angels.

He will punish those who do not know God and do not obey the gospel of our Lord Jesus. They will be punished with everlasting destruction and shut out from the presence of the Lord and from the majesty of his power" (2 Thessalonians 1:7–9).

The *when* of punishment is the end of time, when Christ comes back.

The *what* of punishment is separation from God's awesome and wonderful presence. A lake of burning sulfur is a picture of why hell is *hell*: God isn't there.

The *who* of punishment are those who don't know God—those who haven't received God's offer of forgiveness in Jesus. Accepting that free gift is what it means to "obey the gospel of our Lord Jesus."

Judgment at the End of Time

It's insane for any human being not to know what the Bible teaches about hell.

Hell sounds harsh.

But we wouldn't have it any other way.

Hell shows the evilness of evil. Hell isn't just for Olympians of evil. None of us has a hard time qualifying for the hell team. Jesus tells us who is "outside the city" of heaven: occultists, the sexually immoral, murderers, idolaters, and everyone who loves and practices falsehood (Revelation 22:15). "Idolaters" and "falsehood" catch all of us. But in case you're wondering if you're good enough at being bad, Paul's writings lump together "big" sins with all the "little" sins we're so good at—making it clear that without the forgiveness we gain in Christ, none of us is fit for heaven (Galatians 5:19–21). By the hugeness of the punishment we can gauge the hugeness of our crimes.

Hell displays the rightness of God. So long as sin is allowed to go on, we're likely to see it as no big deal. We're likely to see God as a doof, a stupid old fool. And that would be silly on our part. His perfect love and perfect knowledge roll together to give him perfect judgment (Revelation 16:5–7).

Hell fulfills justice. No sin is hidden from God. At the end of time murderers will no longer go free. Abusers will be found out. All the ghastliness of our hearts will be revealed. Bad guys big and small will fall when God pays back trouble to those who dish it out (2 Thessalonians 1:6).

Hell gives us patience. Evil triumphs ten thousand times a day in your world. Know what? Whatever grief you get for being a Christian—for acting, thinking, and feeling the way God wants you to—will be paid back. God sees. He's on your side. He may take longer to punish evil than you like, but his judgment *will* come (2 Peter 2:9).

Hell confirms our freedom. Now, that's freaky. But it's true.

It's Your Choice

The Bible is clear that God's wrath comes because of a *choice*. God has made himself obvious through the world he has made—so we have no excuse. Hell gives us eternity for what we've chosen in this life: a long walk away from God (Romans 1:18–31). Like Billy Graham has said, "God will never send anybody to hell. If man goes to hell, he goes by his own free choice. Hell was created for the devil and his angels, not for man. God never meant that man should go there." Dante, the huge medieval author of the *Divine Comedy*, wrote, "If you insist on having your own way, you will get it. Hell is the enjoyment of your own way forever."

Hell is a choice because God offers us a way out—a way out of judgment, a way out of the banishment from his presence that makes hell *hell*.

How do you choose that way out?

Admit that you've rebelled. "For all have sinned and fall short of the glory of God" (Roman 3:23). Tell God you've sinned.

Accept God's terms of surrender. "For the wages of sin is death, but the gift of God is eternal life in Christ Jesus our Lord" (Romans 6:23). Tell God you know that Christ died in your place—he died even though *you* are the one who deserves death.

Ask God for his new life. "I tell you the truth, whoever hears my word and believes him who sent me has eternal life and will not be condemned; he has crossed over from death to life" (John 5:24). Tell God thanks for forgiving you and for filling you with power to live a life on *his* side of the cosmic battle.

Your new life can begin now. It's your choice. And being close to him lasts forever.

"Hope is definitely not the same
thing as optimism.
It is not the conviction
that something will turn out well,
but the certainty that
something makes sense,
regardless of how it turns out. "

Václav Havel (b. 1936)
Czech playwright and president
Disturbing the Peace

8

Where Are We Through All of This?

Jesus sure *said* weird stuff. Like that it's easier to shove a camel spitting and kicking through a needle's eye than to squeeze a rich man into heaven. Or that if you cling tight to your life you'll lose it. Jesus once told a mountainside of people that the meek would win the earth. And another time he said religious leaders were like Jeffrey Dahmer's fridge—scrubbed clean on the outside, full of dead bones on the inside.

Jesus *did* weird stuff too. He hocked on the ground, mixed up a mudcake, and rubbed it in a blind guy's eyes—and made him see. Called a dear dead friend back to life after four rottin' days. Ordered a horde of demons into a herd of pigs—which then did a cliff dive. And he invited prostitutes and Israelite IRS agents to parties.

But stop and ponder: The wildest, weirdest thing Jesus ever did was to claim He would return.

Even most pagans admit Jesus was a good man who lived and died, although they argue he stayed good and dead. Most Christians, though, can list at least a few historical proofs why we think Christ rose from the dead, so our belief in a dead man popping from the grave doesn't mean we've unplugged our brains.

But how can we be sure that Christ will come back? Or know exactly what his "second coming" will look like?

Settling the Big Stuff

Believing that Jesus will return to earth doesn't make us wackos from Waco. Or fanatic *hyoo-go*ers. Or Bopponaut wannabees. We have *evidence*. And we're working hard to get *clarity*.

- God's prophets accurately foresaw a slew of details about Christ's *first* coming. That gives us strong assurance we can trust biblical promises about the end of the world. We have wads of detail spoken by Jesus— Mr. Honesty—about his *return*.
- The two basic points of what the Bible teaches about the end of the world are unmistakably clear. God wins. Satan loses. Read it again: Jesus triumphs—and the devil and his horde get served up on toast.
- The outline of key end-time events also seems sure: Birthpains—Great Distress—Christ's Coming—Judgment—Eternity. Bible-obeying Christians do argue about exactly how Christ's second coming plays out— back to that in a minute—but many would agree that these five elements reflect what God's Word predicts.
- Plenty of preachers have wandered past the clear teachings of the Bible—picking antichrists and hyping dates for Christ's coming. That doesn't mean it's impossible to stay within the Bible's boundaries—that is, if we read to obey, read no more or less than what the Bible actually says, and read for the big points. Their *abuse* of Scripture doesn't rule out our responsible *use* of Scripture.

A Couple Huge Questions

But even with those major things settled, a couple questions burn in our brains: 1) *Where will we be* when all this happens? and 2) *When* will all this happen?

First question first—second question next chapter.

A mammoth majority of Christian books about the end of the world focus heavily on the *timing* of Christ's second coming. In one way, that focus couldn't be cooler. Jesus is the big deal. If world history is a water fight, his return is bigger than a Super Soaker plugged straight to the spigot. He's the fire hose of all time. But most of the books sold today teach a distinct understanding of Jesus' return—one that makes too big a point of a single question: *Where will we be when the world ends?*

Here's the indisputable biblical fact: When Jesus returns, he will pull his people to himself. We've already read what Jesus had to say about this gathering:

> At that time the sign of the Son of Man will appear in the sky, and all the nations of the earth will mourn. They will see the Son of Man coming on the clouds of the sky, with power and great glory. And he will send his angels with a loud trumpet call, and they will gather his elect from the four winds, from one end of the heavens to the other.
>
> Matthew 24:30–31

And here's a key passage from the apostle Paul's writings:

> Brothers, we do not want you to be ignorant about those who fall asleep [those who die], or to grieve like the rest of men, who have no hope. We believe that Jesus died and rose again and so we believe that God will bring with Jesus those who have fallen asleep in him. According to the Lord's own word, we tell you that we who are still alive, who are left till the coming of the Lord, will cer-

tainly not precede those who have fallen asleep. For the Lord himself will come down from heaven, with a loud command, with the voice of the archangel and with the trumpet call of God, and the dead in Christ will rise first. After that, we who are still alive and are left will be caught up together with them in the clouds to meet the Lord in the air. And so we will be with the Lord forever.

1 Thessalonians 4:13–17

Jesus promised that when he comes he will "gather his elect . . . from one end of the heavens to the other." Paul wanted the Thessalonians to be clear that Jesus is coming for *all* of God's people—dead or alive. With an ear-shattering shout, Jesus will come down from heaven. The bodies of Christians who have died will rise first. (Most Christians believe their *spirits* have arrived in heaven immediately after death—see Luke 23:43.) Then Christians who are still alive will "be caught up together with them in the clouds to meet the Lord in the air."

When Jesus returns for his own, his people will be "caught up" to meet him. To use the popular Bible prophecy vocab, believers will be "raptured." While the word "rapture" doesn't appear in Scripture, the idea is certainly there—it's from the Latin word *rapio*, which in turn translates the Greek *harpazo*, the word for "caught up."

The Ride of Your Life

The Rapture is a ride guaranteed to satisfy the most savage roller coaster animal. It'll be an up-to-the-sky-high *faahwang*—major bungee jump recoil. *Look, Mom, no hands!* Like the great Christian devotional writer Oswald Chambers once said, "I do not know how I am going to stay up 'in the air' with the Lord, but that is no business of mine."

The *what* of the Rapture usually isn't in question. The

how we may puzzle about. But it's the *when* that people really debate: whether Jesus will come to collect Christians *before, during,* or *after* the Tribulation, that time frame we've called the Great Distress.

Don't get mixed up: This is a different question than how to understand the millennium, that thousand-year period mentioned in Revelation 20. People can be *pre*mil (Jesus comes before the millennium), *post*mil (Jesus comes after the millennium), or *a*mil (Jesus don't need Han Solo's Millennium Falcon to land on earth).

This question is all about the relationship of the Rapture to the Tribulation.

- "Pre-tribulationists" (pre-tribbers) believe Christ will rapture the church *before* the Tribulation.
- "Mid-tribulationists" (mid-tribbers) think Christians will face the first half of the Tribulation, but will be snatched out at a mid-point *during* the Tribulation— before God begins to dump his bowls of wrath. *Big point:* In both the pre-trib and mid-trib views, the Rapture and Christ's second coming are separate events.
- "Post-tribulationists" (post-tribbers) believe Christ will come in a single event at the end of—*after*—the Tribulation.
- "Pan-tribulationists" (pan-tribbers) believe this whole debate is deadly to brain cells and joke that "it will all pan out in the end." (That's a joke. You don't need to remember that one. It won't be on any test.)

Whole books are written on this when-does-the-Rapture-happen question. Oodles of books. Since the subject is so huge and since the teachings of pre-tribbers and post-tribbers are the most common—and the most different— we'll limit our look to those views.

Pre-trib Rapture

Most pre-tribbers hold to several core beliefs. They teach that

- God has promised, they say, to keep the church "from the hour of trial that is going to come upon the whole world" (Revelation 3:10).
- The Rapture will happen as an event *prior* to the Great Distress. The Rapture is a grand happening *separate* from the revealing of Jesus at the end of time.
- The Antichrist can rise to power only *after* the church has been removed from earth. Some believe that God's Holy Spirit living within the church must exit before the Antichrist can be revealed as the "abomination that causes desolation." In other words, God raptures the church out of the way *before* that Antichrist's debut at the beginning of the Great Distress (2 Thessalonians 2:7).
- The believers mentioned in the back half of Revelation are Jews who have become Christians during the Tribulation—not the church.
- The Rapture will be a surprise. Christ will come for his own "like a thief in the night. While people are saying, 'Peace and safety,' destruction will come on them suddenly, as labor pains on a pregnant woman, and they will not escape" (1 Thessalonians 5:2–3).
- The Birthpains show up as a short, dark time immediately before the Rapture—and so they show us when the Rapture is near.

The upside of the pre-tribulation viewpoint is *a strong emphasis on readiness, rooted in an expectation that Christ could return at any moment.* Pre-tribbers see the Sign of Hope we've looked at—God's Good News will be preached to all nations before the end comes. They agree with the Sign of Horror—that the Great Distress will start when the Antichrist is revealed. But they also see a third indication of the end—the Rapture of the church. For pre-tribbers, the Rapture is *the* sign that the end of the world is near. Jesus pulls the pin; seven years (and one Tribulation) later the world blows.

The pre-trib view in a nutshell:

Most important job:
Since Christ could return at any moment, a Christian's *job du jour* is to *be ready—fit to fly*.

Biggest fear:
to be *left behind* to face the Tribulation.

Biggest weakness:
"escapism"—the feeling that God will snatch you out of every ugliness of life.

Favorite bumper sticker:
"See you here, there, or in the air."

Pre-tribber's order of end-time events:
Birthpains—*Rapture*—Great Distress—Second Coming—Judgment—Eternity.

Post-trib Rapture
Anyone with half a brain would prefer the pre-tribulation view to be correct. For post-tribbers, that's the problem. Pre-trib ideas are too good to be true. Post-tribbers teach that

• God will protect Christians *through* the Great Distress,

not *from* it. Living through the tribulation won't be as casual as sitting around watching fireworks; Christians will suffer through horrible human-made hassles but be protected from God's wrath. (Believers get God's seal of protection in Revelation 7:3 and 9:4. And it seems that the one way out of the Tribulation is martyrdom—Revelation 7:14; 20:4. The price of a ticket out seems way high.) Related point: Revelation 3:10, they say, was a promise to just the church in Philadelphia.

- The believers we spot on earth during Revelation are *the church*, not just Jews who have become Christians. (This point is part of a complicated theological spat—may seem minor, but very important.)
- The Rapture and Second Coming are one event. Jesus' words clearly link his *appearing, judgment* of the nations, and *gathering* of believers all in one breath (Matthew 24:30–32). Christ's coming is like picking up a fumbled football and running it into the end zone—an all-at-once big deal.
- The pre-tribbers assume that "a church a day keeps the Antichrist away," based on 2 Thessalonians 2:7. They teach that the church (or the Holy Spirit in the church) is what holds him back—that the church must be raptured for evil to flourish. At best, that's a guess. It's not in the verse. Read it for yourself.
- The pre-trib rapture position is relatively new. The church historically has taught a post-trib position.
- The long chunks of Scripture that talk about the end times—Matthew 24–25 and the book of Revelation—never explicitly mention a two-tango return. Nor does any other scripture. The pre-trib argument for a "secret coming" of Jesus to rapture believers must be a real secret!

The upside of the post-trib viewpoint is *the burning de-*

sire to be strong enough to face the toughest of trials with Christ's strength. While pre-tribbers believe Jesus could come at any moment, post-tribbers think we'll see the Antichrist and the Great Distress first.

The post-trib view in a nutshell:

Most important job:
Since Christ won't return until after the Tribulation, a Christian's most important job is to *be tough* in hard times.

Biggest fear:
being *too weak* to face the trials ahead.

Biggest weakness:
being sellers of gloom and doom.

Favorite bumper sticker:
"Hope for the best. Prepare for the worst."

And another one:
"If I'm wrong, I'll apologize when we fly in the sky."

Post-tribber's order of end-time events:
Birthpains—Great Distress—Second Coming *and Rapture*—Judgment—Eternity.

So What's the Scoop?
Whatever you think about the timing of the Great Scoop, there are some facts of life you can be sure of:

We do suffer. God isn't a divine caddie who steers Christians clear of life's every sand trap and water hazard. Jesus said it plainly: "In this world you will have trouble. But take heart! I have overcome the world" (John 16:33).

We do suffer greatly. Whoever the believers are in Revelation—saved Jews or the Gentile church—they pay the ultimate price for their faith. So do many Christians today. There is *never* a guarantee in the Bible that God will unfailingly snatch us from persecution or any other nastiness of life.

We won't suffer beyond what we can bear. Remember? God has cut short the Great Distress for the sake of his people. We won't be tempted beyond what we can handle. Here's a hint, though: Don't picture God as a kindergarten teacher who wants everything easy, rosy, and happy. Think of him as a rocket-science professor who blows your brain way past what you thought were its limits. Grow for it.

We don't suffer God's wrath. Bad has a limit for believers. God doesn't beat up his buddies. The Bible is clear: "For God did not appoint us to suffer wrath but to receive salvation through our Lord Jesus Christ" (1 Thessalonians 5:9). And that verse shows up in the context of God whacking evil at the end of time.

So What Color Are the Bathrooms in Your Church Basement?

Don't freak. Don't fret. Everyone agrees that Jesus is going to come back and swoop us home, even if we do debate—loudly—the timing of the Rapture.

You have to put this on a scale of 1 to 10 of "things worth pondering." A biggie question like how we're made right with God is definitely a *10*—better get the answer straight. What color to paint the bathrooms in your church basement is a *1*—despite the fact that churches have split over seafoam green vs. robin's egg blue. Things like forms of baptism, gifts of the spirit, and free will vs. determinism might be a *6* or *7*—not a matter of whether you're a Christian or not, but biggish in how you run your Christian life.

So how important is the *timing* of the Rapture? In the grand scheme of things, probably about a *3*. Watch out for people who make it a *10*.

And there's one fact about the Rapture you can be indubitably sure of: Knowing where Christians are during the events of the end isn't the great question of life. It's nice to predict we'll be in heaven. It's probably smart to brace to be on earth. But more important than where *we* are is where *you* are.

Sooner or later we'll get to heaven—all of us: pre-trib, mid-trib, post-trib—as it really does all pan out in the end.

Where will you be?

It's your choice whose side you'll stand on. And which spot you'll spend eternity in.

You can be *with* the Toaster.

Or *in* the toaster.

"The cleverest of all,
in my opinion, is the man
who calls himself a fool
at least once a month."

Feodor Dostoyevsky (1821-1881)
Russian novelist
A Writer's Diary

9

Are We There Yet?

Don't miss these "too hot to handle" Bible prophecies your government supposedly wants to shush up:

- The Antichrist is alive—and living in the United States. He's an ultra-wealthy businessman building a private army of thought-control experts and satanic missionaries. He'll begin his assault "any day now."
- By 1998, some 200 million Americans will wear the mark of the beast.
- Several signs *prove* that the world is rushing to The End—AIDS, a sudden rise in earthquakes and volcanic activity, flooding in the U.S., the fall of the Soviet Union, and the return of Jews to Israel after World War II.
- The battle of Armageddon will start on May 3, 2000—and the world will go *kablooey* ten days later. Mark your calendar with a big E.O.W. for May 13, 2000. (Looks like God wants to spare the class of double zero from final exams.)
- And all these facts are being suppressed by the CIA, FBI, and White House in "a conspiracy calculated to

rob Americans of their spiritual free will." The CIA and FBI are telling prophecy scholars to keep quiet in an effort to keep the country calm.

Bunches of books, videos, tabloids, teachers, and preachers say the human race is flaming toward its end—including the tab *Weekly World News,* the source of these claims dug from the book *Paradise Waiting: What You MUST Do to Live Forever.*

Jesus is coming. Not *someday,* they say. Not even *soon.* He'll show up *immediately.*

Maybe.

Or maybe not.

Maybe this is the chapter you've been waiting for. You want to know whether all this stuff is ready to happen *right now.* Whether you need to rearrange your life schedule for the year 2000—or 2005. Whether you can shred your school books—or whether you'd better study for finals.

Jesus is coming back. That's settled.

But when is lift-off? Now? Later? Long after we're dead and gone?

It's the bazillion-dollar question: When will the toast be tasty?

The Great Date Wait

The questions have burned for two thousand years. When will Jesus come back? What's up with the Antichrist? Doth we dangle on the edge of the Great Distress?

It's what the disciples asked just before Jesus died. They snuck up to Jesus and said, " 'Tell us . . . what will be the sign of your coming and of the end of the age?' " (Matthew 24:3). Moments before Jesus ascended to heaven, the disciples snooped some more: "So when they met together, they asked him, 'Lord, are you at this time going to restore the kingdom to Israel?' " (Acts 1:6).

Those questions still burn. We want answers. Details. A map of the road ahead.

It's like being on a family vacation. Say your family misplaces itself somewhere between Missoula and Memphis. What happens? Dad bangs his head on the steering wheel. Mom whips out the map. The kids shriek that universal cry of bored backsides: ARE WE THERE YET?

As Christians, we know where we're headed—heaven—but we don't know *all* the points along the way. Not exactly, anyway. We've whipped out the map—the Bible—and figured out which way is up. Even so, it's hard to stop the backseat sobs: ARE WE THERE YET?

Right now a *lot* of books offer quick answers. And they offer pretty much the same assortment of reasons why *now*—as in *the next few years*, at the longest—is the time Jesus will return:

- God's Good News of Jesus will soon be preached to the whole world—and like Jesus said, "then the end will come."
- Worse-than-ever natural disasters and extreme evil confirm that we are living in earth's final days.
- The rise of a worldwide culture and economy—coupled with the invention of screamingly fast computers and other new technologies—has prepared the way for the Antichrist to build his all-controlling, all-present government.
- The rebirth of Israel as a nation is conclusive proof that the end is here.

Serious claims.

So are the answers that cut through the hype.

Everybody Hears about Jesus

It's the Sign of Hope: Before the end of time "this gospel of the kingdom will be preached in the whole world" (Matthew 24:14). That job seems within reach.

But predicting Christ's coming by our "completing the missionary task" is tricky. What Jesus meant by "preached in the whole world" isn't totally clear. The words he used mean "to all peoples." Does that mean establishing churches in every "people group"? Preaching to every household? To every person? Or is it even something more supernatural—the angels in Revelation swooping down with the message of God?

And one hitch: Jesus said this Sign of Hope is *preceded* by bloody persecutions and a massive ditching of faith. It's scary stuff: "Then you will be handed over to be persecuted and put to death, and you will be hated by *all nations* because of me. At that time many will turn away from the faith and will betray and hate each other, and many false prophets will appear and deceive many people. Because of the increase of wickedness, the love of most will grow cold" (italics added; Matthew 24:9–12).

Right now persecution *is* raging around the world. Still, *many* Christians have had reason to believe their deadly suffering meant the end was near—in times and places all the way from the early church to twentieth-century China to the Soviet Union.

So don't celebrate a job-well-done just yet. At the least, our confidence that we can reach the world needs to be tempered by an awareness of what it will cost us.

Ugly Days Are Here Again

The Jesus-will-be-here-today-after-lunch crowd claims that the world is facing unprecedented disasters—sure signs, they say, of Christ's immediate arrival. How so? They interpret the Birthpains as a short time of crisis just prior to Christ's coming again. And they claim the current pain in our world is beyond a doubt the awful stuff Jesus predicted.

Problem Number One: Though the Birthpains *could* be a relatively brief, ugly time, Jesus said those events indicate "the end is still to come," literally "the end is not yet" (Matthew 24:6).

Then there's Problem Number Two: History proves we *aren't* living in the worst of all possible worlds. Get a grip on these deaths caused by earthquake, famine, and disease:

Killer quakes. The January 1995 Kobe earthquake left 45,000 Japanese dead. But in 1975, some 240,000 were killed in Tangshan, China. Add to those another 137,000 in Hokkaido, Japan, on December 30, 1730, and a whopping 300,000 in Calcutta, India, on October 11, 1737. And a quake on January 24, 1556, in Shaanxi, China, killed a mind-boggling *830,000* people. The point? Even if Los Angeles slid into the ocean tomorrow it wouldn't necessarily prove the end is here.

Withering starvation. Maybe you sponsor a hungry child somewhere on the planet. No doubt that he or she needs your help! But researchers list some 400 catastrophic famines in human history—and that's just in *recorded* history. A sample of the pain: Ten million people starved in India in 1769–1770, and about another ten million during 1877–1878 in northern China. Famine caused by war killed well over three million in China's Henan Province in 1943, and famine in Russia took five million lives in 1921–22.

Deadly disease. AIDS is bad. Ebola is bloody. Flesh-eating bacteria are for real. But need an example of a *real* plague? The Black Death swept across Europe in the mid-fourteenth century, killing as much as three quarters of the population in less than twenty years. We're still here.

So what's up? All these wild claims that today's disasters are uniquely dire are products of an when-I-was-little-the-snow-was-up-to-here effect. It's an arrogant, ignorant attitude that what our generation has experienced is the world's deepest, highest, worstest, bestest, biggest, smallest, fastest, slowest . . . you get the idea.

Extreme Evil

Many writers also assert we live in times more evil than any other period of history—what they see as a fulfillment of Paul's words to Timothy about the last days: "There will be terrible times in the last days. People will be lovers of themselves, lovers of money, boastful, proud, abusive, disobedient to their parents, ungrateful, unholy, without love, unforgiving, slanderous, without self-control, brutal, not lovers of the good, treacherous, rash, conceited, lovers of pleasure rather than lovers of God" (2 Timothy 3:1–4).

Again, time for a reality check: Hit the history books and ponder the worlds of hate, family discord, immorality, and ungodliness created by the likes of Adolf Hitler, Josef Stalin, and Pol Pot. Don't dishonor the dead with your whining. To claim our world is awash in the worst evil ever is like a man with a pebble in his shoe complaining to a man who has no feet.

Worldwide Everything

Look through your closet. At the back panels of your home computer, TV, VCR, or CD player. At the tag on your shoes. Your stuff is made in places you may not even have heard of. And for every something shipped here, we've shipped something there—from Michael Jackson to McDonald's. Our economy is going global. Cultures around the world share, borrow, and blend. And some even call for the

United Nations to be a more powerful body spearheading a "New World Order."

The effect? Many writers claim this "McWorld" you live in is ripe for the Antichrist to take control through a one-world government, economy, and religion.

The Antichrist's rise to power is even more certain, they say, because today's technology gives him the ability to control every human being on the planet. Computers, on-line banking, debit cards, and supermarket checkout scanners, for example, will enable the government to track your every purchase, creating a cashless society where you can't buy or sell without the Beast's mark—no doubt a supersmart chip implanted in your forehead or hand. And holograms will let the Antichrist project his living image around the world.

Here's the trick: Technology doesn't equate with evil. Dictators have never needed computers to prohibit buying and selling, and technology alone can't stamp out cow-swapping if cash goes the way of stone coins. In a day when the IRS can't even properly cross-check people's tax returns, it's not likely that armies of bureaucrats are swiveling in their chairs thinking, *Hmm . . . let's use computers to control who buys Tupperware and Twinkies.* Even Bill Gates doesn't think that big.

Here's another trick: Unity doesn't equate with evil. End-time writers fear that European Union—which may still whimper into nothingness—will be the Beast's platform for power. A "United States of Europe," they say, will be the confederacy of nations that allows him to seize worldwide control. But if unity is always evil, then the one-government, one-currency union of the United States of America should have ushered in the Antichrist a couple hundred years ago. And if multinational unity is always bad, then perhaps the Allies should have let Hitler conquer the planet.

We may be awed by technological progress. We may be

scared to live in a multicultural world. But the rapid changes we see don't mean the Antichrist is a rich man living in America ready to grab control. The Bible foresees a time we almost can't imagine. From the jungles of Java to the urban concrete of America, *everyone* is aware of the Beast. *Everyone* is controlled. *Everyone* is presented with a clear choice between Christ and Antichrist. That's the *real* New World Order. And our growing governments and technology may not have anything to do with it.

Born-Again Israel

For end-of-the-world preachers and writers, the rebirth of Israel as a nation outproves all other proofs that the world will stop spinning tomorrow. They almost universally claim that when the Jews regained their land—when Israel once again became a country in 1948—a quick countdown to the end of the world began. It's the surest signal we have, they say, that the end is not just *near*, but *here*.

There's one key Bible passage behind their hype: Jesus said, "Now learn this lesson from the fig tree: As soon as its twigs get tender and its leaves come out, you know that summer is near. Even so, when you see all these things, you know that it is near, right at the door. I tell you the truth, this generation will certainly not pass away until all these things have happened" (Matthew 24:32–34).

Those verses, they say, tell us three things: 1) The fig tree is Israel's rebirth in its former land. 2) This rebirth signals that the end of all things is near. 3) The generation of people alive at the time won't die before all of Jesus' predictions about the end of the world come true.

Maybe not.

The rebirth of Israel maybe isn't the egg timer that will tell us when we'll all be hard boiled. Hang tight and learn why:

- It's *totally* squishing the fig to say the fig tree symbol-izes Israel's rebirth as a political kingdom. The Bible most often uses the fig tree as a symbol of a time when life is hip and happy—when God rules and everyone dwells in his peace (check out 1 Kings 4:25 and Micah 4:4 for examples). It's Hebrew shorthand, something like our phrase "American Dream." Say those words and everyone pictures a house with a white picket fence, a two-car garage, a dog, and two-and-a-half chil-dren. The fig isn't a figure for political statehood.
- But even that Happy Hour at the Fig Tree Grill isn't what Jesus is talking about here. The same passage in Luke 21:29 reports that Jesus added the phrase "all the trees." If he was trying to talk about Israel, he really botched his punch line. He could just as well have said "when the apple tree blossoms" or "when the corn grows tall." He wasn't trying to *wink-wink-nudge-nudge* us some secret message about Israel.
- Here's the important point: What the fig tree clearly refers to *here* is the arrival of *"all these things."* Jesus is saying that when the human race has seen the arrival of the Antichrist, the Great Distress, and even his ap-pearing in the clouds—*then* the end is near. *Then* we can be sure. *Then* the generation that sees these things will surely witness "the end of the age."

Tens of millions of books—and that's no exaggeration—have taught that Jesus would come within a generation of the rebirth of Israel in 1948. And they pegged the length of a biblical generation at forty years.

Do the math. Jesus should have shown up a decade or more ago.

The year 1988 came and went. Even so, the idea of "he'll come back within a generation of Israel's statehood" persists. Just when 1998 comes and goes and 200 million American's aren't wearing the mark of the beast—and everyone figures out that *that* pack of predictions was wrong—another preacher pops up to make more way-out claims.

Answering all these claims is a little like proving Elvis isn't alive. Digging up his body and putting his head on display wouldn't satisfy some folks. And looking at the clear teaching of the Bible won't shut up some of these soothsayers.

But What Does the Bible Really Say?

Want the real truth about the Bible's time for the end of the world? Lotsa folks admit we can't know the *time* or *date* of Christ's coming—but they're happy to peg a *month* or *year*. Or at least pinpoint the next few years as the certain *season* of his coming.

Lotsa folks say the Bible guarantees believers some knowledge about the timing of Christ's coming—that we won't be caught by surprise. They quote Paul's words: "But you, brothers, are not in darkness so that this day should surprise you like a thief. You are all sons of the light and sons of the day. We do not belong to the night or to the darkness" (1 Thessalonians 5:4–5).

What Paul means, though, isn't that we will *know* the time but that we should *be ready* at any time. Paul goes on to say that being "of the light" means to be "self-controlled, putting on faith and love as a breastplate, and the hope of salvation as a helmet" (1 Thessalonians 5:8). We shouldn't be caught doing wrong—like the burglar in the house who gets plugged full of lead when the owner flips on the light.

Yet lotsa folks still say we *know* Jesus is coming soon.

That's strange, considering Jesus said over and over we

won't know: "No one knows about that day or hour, not even the angels in heaven, nor the Son, but only the Father" (Matthew 24:36). "Be on guard! Be alert! You do not know when that time will come" (Mark 13:33). "Therefore keep watch, because you do not know on what day your Lord will come" (Matthew 24:42). "It is not for you to know the times or dates the Father has set by his own authority" (Acts 1:7).

Jesus said *nonbelievers* will be clueless about his coming. Back in the time of Noah, sinful people ". . . knew nothing about what would happen until the flood came and took them all away. That is how it will be at the coming of the Son of Man" (Matthew 24:39). But even *followers* of Jesus will be surprised: "So *you* also must be ready, because the Son of Man will come at an hour when *you* do not expect him" (italics added; Matthew 24:44).

You get the point.

We don't know when Christ will come again. But that's still not the end of the story.

"I make known the end
from the beginning,
from ancient times,
what is still to come.
I say: My purpose will stand,
and I will do all that I please."

The prophet Isaiah
Isaiah 46:10

10

Since the World Is Spinning Down

Maybe you've figured it out: Interpreting Bible prophecy is a lot like reading a doctor's office eye chart. Just about everyone can see the big E. The next few lines are pretty clear too. Squint and maybe you can read further. But then the doc tells you to keep reading. If you're honest, after a while you have to say, "I don't know." Or you see what you want to see. Or you just start making up letters.

Truth in Advertising

You don't want to be sold a pile of hooey by this book or any other. You want to understand the *sure* things about the end of the world—so you don't scamper out on shaky limbs of *speculation* or *skepticism*. So sit tight for a page and read a bit of fine print. Then we'll look at one last gargantuan fact about the end of time.

Here's a fact you need to know: Bible students don't always agree even on the big letters at the top of the chart. Some scholars argue that all of Jesus' words in Matthew 24 were fulfilled within a few decades of his crucifixion. There's partial truth in what they say. Jesus *was* making a two-pronged prediction. One point predicted events of Israel's near future, like the fall of Jerusalem in A.D. 70. But this school o' thought ignores the more important point, that Jesus clearly was previewing the finish of the planet—telling us about an ultimate Antichrist, his own bodily second coming, and God's final judgment of the human race.

Conclusion? Either Jesus is really mixed up—or the scholars are. Go ahead and cast your vote. But don't bet against the guy with the bigger brain.

Reading Revelation is even less tidy than sorting through Jesus' teaching. Most scholars sit in one of four main camps:

- Some scholars of Revelation (called "preterists") think that the book's bizarre visions describe events that took place in the first century—the same slant they put on Jesus' words. They say almost everything in the book reflects the persecutions and victories Christians experienced shortly after Christ first walked the earth.
- Others ("historicists") argue that the contents of the book lay out in advance the whole of church history—that the events of the book can be matched to the church's goings-on of the last two thousand years.
- Yet another group ("idealists") gives up on the goo of symbols—they say the book is a psychedelic picture of good battling evil.
- A fourth view ("futurist") is the one most widely accepted today among Bible-believing Christians—admittedly with some wide variations in interpretation. The teaching of *Look Who's Toast Now!* is basically futurist.

There's truth in each view, though you have to do quite a wedgie on church history to make the historicist view work. But the bulk of Revelation is clear: It describes the future completion of God's kingdom. One clue? Revelation itself says early on that it's a mix both of what was present and what would be future. Christ told John the apostle to write "what you have seen, what is now and what will take place later" (1:19).

Fine Print at the Ad's Bottom

It isn't just our own brains that make end of time events misty with mystery. God himself leaves out some of the details. In Revelation 10:3–4, for example, seven thunders "speak," but John is forbidden to write down what they say.

There are other places where we don't get the whole picture:

- We don't know all the details on *events*. It's hardly clear, for example, exactly what happens during the trumpets and bowls, or how they all take place. Are the judgments of Revelation something God works all by himself, or do humans help out?
- We can't always agree on *identity*. Some people argue that the Antichrist isn't a person at all—that he is a force of godless authority, human governments gone mad. Whatever the Beast of Revelation is, he's no dead chunk of chopped liver. He leads the evil charge against God at the end of time.
- It's impossible to perfectly determine *sequence*. A couple puzzles: to what extent the trumpets and bowls overlap, or how the events in Revelation do or don't fall in chronological order.

If you haven't figured it out by now, *Look Who's Toast Now!* focuses on the broad points of Bible prophecy—the big letters at the top of the eye chart, those things Scripture tells us for sure.

You can confirm these things by reading the Bible for

yourself. But beware of one largeo hazardo: Lots of Bible prophecy buffs lock themselves up and "solve" the Bible's puzzles themselves. In fact, the covers of their books often parade how many times they've read the Bible or how many hours they've logged flying solo in the cockpit of Bible study. But bring their "facts" out into the light and they crash. Why? The Bible was written to no single individual. Not to you. Not to any of those authors. So study along with other Christians. Read for the big points. Stick to the core. And learn what your Christian brothers and sisters have believed throughout church history.

Enough said.

Know Your Toaster Facts

Despite these arguments, God's truth about the end of the world boils down to three indisputable, non-debatable, unstoppable truths. The first two you'd better know by now:

End-of-the-World Fact #1

GOD WINS.

End-of-the-World Fact #2

SATAN LOSES.

These aren't someone's iffy interpretation of Bible prophecy, but God's sure promises. They're truth to live by. But these first two End-of-the-World Facts don't tell you everything you need to know to set your life straight. There's a third fact to figure out.

It's True. Now What?

So now what do you do?

If these facts really are true, then they affect how you live till the end of time.

Big problem: We don't see Jesus just yet. But our brains

think in categories of *now* or *never*. Jesus is either coming this afternoon or not at all. As you face the end it's easy to get grabbed by an antsy, wet-your-pants-with-excitement *right now*. Or to buy into a forget-about-Jesus *never*.

Wrong Way to Face the End #1: Check Out

If you are *abzolootly pozitootly* convinced that Jesus will show up by the end of the day—or the end of this decade or next—what are you likely to do? It'd be tempting to sit around and skywatch. To exit reality. To make no long-term life plans—or feel guilty and unspiritual if you do.

Imagine your principal firing up the intercom one Monday and announcing that sometime soon—no later than Friday—school will slam shut. Permanently. The whole thing, however, is a steal of a deal. You'll get your diploma. Guaranteed. Only condition? You have to stick around to pick it up.

Be honest. Where's your head for the next few hours and days? You show for class but don't take notes. You cover your eyes to write exams and mark multichoice quiz questions willy-nilly. All you chat about with your friends is how great it will be to get your sheepskin.

Cruel surprise. The school board decides to keep your school open. They grade your tests and tell you you flunked. You're worse than sunk.

Get this clue: Despite claims to the contrary, life is still in session. And if we don't know when Jesus is coming, then checking out isn't prudent.

Wrong Way to Face the End #2: Run Wild

Second scenario: A student gets on the intercom and squawks that the whole school administration has just left. For good. He says you have free run of the school. Free run of life, in fact.

The choices get really rude when you think there are no consequences to your actions, no judge around to execute judgment. You could smoke pot in the stairwells. Or hotwire a janitor's cart and hurl through the lunchroom. Or just ditch class because you don't give a rip.

Cruel joke. The principal is back and you're gonna be sorry. *Heh lah, heh lah, the big boy's back.*

Get another clue: God exists. Jesus may be a long time coming, but he *will* return. Judgment and joy truly are coming.

The Right Way to Face the End

Now—as in *this instant*—isn't likely the time of Jesus' return. *Never*—as in *not at all*—is a lie. If we want to pinpoint Jesus' time of arrival, we'd have to say it's sometime between now and never. If checking out or running wild aren't appropriate responses to that news, then what?

Jesus said to "be ready, because the Son of Man will come at an hour when you do not expect him" (Matthew 24:44). He said to "keep watch, because you do not know the day or the hour" (Matthew 25:13). He told three stories to explain what it means to "be ready" and to "keep watch." A *wicked servant* who begins to beat his fellow servants while his master is away will be "cut to pieces" (Matthew 24:46–51). *Foolish virgins* who let their lamps go out before the groom returns get locked out of the wedding hall (Matthew 25:1–13). And a *lazy servant* who refuses to use what he has to serve his master is tossed into the darkness to weep and gnash teeth (Matthew 25:14–30).

Sounds like being wicked, foolish, or lazy isn't in God's plan for you as you await the end. He has a better way:

End of the World Fact #3
BELIEVERS LOOK FORWARD AND LIVE HOLY.

Check what Peter wrote about looking forward and God's way to live. It sums up what Jesus taught about being ready and keeping watch:

> But the day of the Lord will come like a thief. The heavens will disappear with a roar; the elements will be destroyed by fire, and the earth and everything in it will be laid bare. Since everything will be destroyed in this way, what kind of people ought you to be? You ought to live holy and godly lives as you look forward to the day of God and speed its coming. That day will bring about the destruction of the heavens by fire, and the elements will melt in the heat. But in keeping with his promise we are looking forward to a new heaven and a new earth, the home of righteousness. So then, dear friends, since you are looking forward to this, make every effort to be found spotless, blameless and at peace with him.
>
> 2 Peter 3:10–14

Peter is talking about an attitude of confident faith: You can look forward to the final overthrow of evil—and to an eternal home where God's sweet will is done every day in every way. Faith in those facts should burst from your brain into your life: You can live a holy and godly life—spotless, blameless, and at peace with God.

Got the picture? Christ's return *someday* doesn't make you good-for-nothing or bad-at-everything. It motivates you *now* to live a holy, patient, persevering life as you wait for him.

Our Savior Is Back

Jesus isn't looking for a welcome-home party—not the kind we'd throw for an astronaut back from the moon or

Mars. He's not stumping for a hero's welcome from a bunch of adoring strangers. He's returning to pick up all of us who belong to him.

"Looking forward" may sound cool and easy. "Living holy" may sound dull and backbreaking. It's not so scary. It's what you look like when you're on God's side. Peter put it this way: "Make every effort to add to your faith goodness; and to goodness, knowledge; and to knowledge, self-control; and to self-control, perseverance; and to perseverance, godliness; and to godliness, brotherly kindness; and to brotherly kindness, love" (2 Peter 1:5–7). If you belong to God, then maturity—holiness, godliness, spotlessness, blamelessness, peace, and all that other stuff—is how God wants to grow you as you wait for him.

You're found totally "spotless, blameless, and at peace with him" when you live in God's forgiveness in Christ—never forgetting that the basis for your friendship with God is Christ's death in your place.

Forgiveness, though, is just the beginning. Forgiveness is fertile dirt that grows you. If you're rooted in forgiveness, exposed to the light of the Holy Spirit, and watered by God's Word—the Bible—you have what you need to grow. You'll live holy.

Fight for Your Future

Satan would like nothing more than for you to waste your life camping in a cornfield, waiting for Jesus to return. Or for you to throw away your life because you think God has left you here to rot. However long you're here—and in any human perspective it's probably a long time rather than short—to "keep watch" and "be ready" means to do what you're supposed to do. To scope out God's long-term will for your life, then act on it.

Jesus may come sooner. That's great.

Jesus may come later. Then you have a great job to do.

People think Christians are hypocrites. And people think Christians are nuns hiding from the world. Hardly. You can show them different. One last word from Peter. He said this: "Live such good lives among the pagans that, though they accuse you of doing wrong, they may see your good deeds and glorify God on the day he visits us" (1 Peter 2:12).

Looking forward and living holy will look different for your generation than for any other. It's gigantic stuff.

To people who think you're a hypocrite, you can showcase love. Your generation can show the world's broken pagans what it looks like to have an intact family—loving your parents, spouse, and kids. You can demonstrate God's love in your community, country, and the whole of human civilization.

To people who think you're a coward, you can go over the walls of your church and show them that Jesus is more than superintendent of Sunday school. Let them know that God is Lord over all. He has answers to the absolutely huge intellectual and social issues coming to challenge the faith of your generation of Christians: euthanasia, cloning, race relations, biochemistry and personality, postmodern thought, artificial intelligence, the age of the universe, the downfall of evolution and the rise of intelligent design.

If you're wise, you'll ponder these things.

Christians in the past were terrified when the earth wasn't flat and the sun didn't revolve around the earth. Today it's technology, change, and world culture that Christians fear. You can cower along with them. Or you and your generation can make long-term, God-pleasing choices to seize the future for Jesus.

An end-times fever that robs you of God's plan for your

life is a deadly infection. A live-for-self flu leaves you and your world coated in vomit.

Look forward.

Live holy.

"Show me, O LORD,
my life's end and the number
of my days;
let me know how fleeting
is my life.
You have made my days a mere
handbreadth; the span of my years
is as nothing before you.
Each man's life is but a breath."

David of Israel (1040-970 B.C.)
Psalm 39:4-5

The End Is Near.
Really.

Get it straight: The end of the world is all about *Jesus*. He's the one behind the Bible's no-doubt-about-'em facts about the future:

God wins. Jesus rides in to reign as King of Kings.

Satan loses. Jesus erases all evil.

Believers look forward and live holy. Jesus comes back for his friends—a people pumped to live forever at his place.

But the end of the world is also about *you.* It's all about your own future.

The Bible won't tell you if you'll play for the Bulls. Or if your Barbie collection will be worth billions. It doesn't say whether your future will look like a blast to *The Jetsons*— or a hellish scene from *Mad Max.* (Reality is usually somewhere in between.)

The Bible does tell you, though, that you'll stand by Jesus' side forever—or spend forever separated from him. When Jesus comes back he'll bring peace to his friends— and judgment to his enemies. Your future is beautiful—or so ugly it should make you scream. Blindingly bright—or as dark as dark gets.

Stupidity Busters

God never meant for you to live clueless about the future.

Without understanding God's plans for wrapping up this world, you'll live in hopelessness. When you feel hurt by life, you'll blame God—not the rebellion that's the real cause of evil in this world. When you think life will never be fair or fun, you'll dread every tomorrow—and forget that God promises an eternity of more fun than you can fathom. When evil constantly succeeds all around you, you'll quit being good—and ignore the fact that God commands you to be faithful to the end. You'll rule your life by whims of what feels good rather than the long-term truth that good triumphs and evil is destroyed. And you'll live without a sense of God's ultimate protection through whatever you face, whenever you face it.

Yet the biggest reason God tells you about the end is so you'll ponder hard your relationship with him. The most important fact you can know about what's ahead is whether *you* spend eternity with *Jesus*.

Signing God's Peace Agreement

Look Who's Toast Now! has unveiled some straightforward Bible truth about your future. You've peered ahead as if the future were past tense.

Maybe you don't like what you saw.

You don't know exactly what it means to be a Christian. . . .

You haven't taken "God stuff" seriously. . . .

You can't swallow the Bible's teachings about The End. . . .

You won't settle down long enough to decide to follow Jesus. . . .

. . . And so you're not sure where you'll spend eternity. Or you do know—and don't want to go.

God doesn't dangle you over the edge of time just to give you a good scare. Bible prophecy isn't an entertaining read—like the big *whew!* you get from a horror flick, the kind that makes real life seem good by comparison. The Bible's teachings about the end of the world aren't a head game—factoids to spit back on a Sunday school test. God expects you to take the knowledge he's given you and *do something* with it.

He wants you to be forever friends with him.

God himself tells us three grand facts of life in this universe that show us how to be friends with him.

1. There's a problem *between us and God: Sin.*

We're rebels.

God's foes.

Mercenaries in the wrong army.

We do bad. We neglect to do good. The Bible's lists of sins and sinners nail all of us: Exodus says *Have no false gods. Don't treat God's name with disrespect. Worship God only. Honor Mom and Dad. Don't murder, sleep around, steal, lie,* or *wish you could* (Exodus 20:1–17). Paul lists *witchcraft, drunkenness, hatred, strife, jealousy, rage, selfish ambition, quarrels* (Galatians 5:19–21). In another spot he includes *greed, bitterness, impurity, sexual wrong, slander, obscenity, dirty jokes* (Ephesians 4:31–5:5). Revelation says *the cowardly, the unbelieving, the vile, the murderers, the sexually immoral, those who practice magic arts, the idolaters, and all liars* will find their place "in the fiery lake of burning sulfur" (Revelation 21:8).

And Jesus points out that you don't have to *do* those

things to be in the wrong—sins of the heart are just as dark (Matthew 5:28).

The truth is that we are *all* sinners: "All have sinned and fall short of the glory of God" (Romans 3:23).

2. God has a solution *to our problem: Christ's death for us on the cross.*

"The wages of sin is death," the Bible says, "but the gift of God is eternal life in Christ Jesus our Lord" (Romans 6:23). God doesn't shrug off sin. Sin erects a wall between us and God—permanent separation from him. It's a pain and loneliness and alienation that starts now and worsens for eternity.

But we don't have to stay far from God.

God's penalty for rebellion is death, yet God's Good News is that Jesus paid the penalty for us. He died a death he didn't deserve. On the cross his agony demonstrated the awfulness of our disobedience for all time. And he bore God's total anger toward a sinful human race.

3. God expects our response: *He wants us to receive him—to change our minds about sin and about him.*

Our response is to accept God's terms of truce—to trust in who Jesus is and what he accomplished for us. These are the terms of the friendship he offers: "To all who received him, to those who believed in his name, he gave the right to become children of God" (John 1:12).

To receive him means we change our minds about sin. God doesn't want us just sorry that his cosmic X-ray vision spotted us sneaky little evildoers. He doesn't want us sorry we got caught, but sorry for the hurt our rebellion has caused ourselves, others, and him. And aware of the wrongness of our wrong.

To receive him means we change our minds about God. We finally admit that God's commands are wholly good, totally kind. That Jesus is God in a bod. That his gift of forgiveness is the one way our sins can be wiped away so we can be accepted by him.

Receiving him might be an attitude of trust and faith that grows over time. Or receiving Christ might happen in a prayer you can pinpoint in time and space—one you can pray right now: "God, I know I've sinned against you. Thank you that Christ died in my place and took the punishment I deserved. Thank you for forgiving me. Help me to follow you." Either way, the result is the same: You start a new life as God's friend.

No More Fear

God rules. Satan roasts. You want to be ready. On the right side. Here's the truth: It doesn't do diddly squat good to be sure of earth's future history if you're unsure of your own destiny.

So admit the *problem*. Trust God's *solution*. Choose God's right *response*.

Deciding to be a Christian—a follower of Jesus—means you're suddenly on God's side. Here's how Jesus described it: "I tell you the truth, whoever hears my word and believes him who sent me has eternal life and will not be condemned; he has crossed over from death to life" (John 5:24). Paul used these cool words: ". . . giving thanks to the Father, who has qualified you to share in the inheritance of the saints in the kingdom of light. For he has rescued us from the dominion of darkness and brought us into the kingdom of the Son he loves, in whom we have redemption, the forgiveness of sins" (Colossians 1:12–14).

Being "reborn" as a Christian is the start of a new relationship with the King of the Universe. You've come back to his kingdom. It's time to start looking forward and living holy.

God wants your relationship with him to grow every day. So get to know God. Find out how to obey him by reading the Bible. Get together with God's people by becoming part of a rock-solid church. And get going on God's plan for your life by picking up books like *Can I Be a Christian Without Being Weird?* (part of a series of books for early teens—published by Bethany House Publishers) or *Catch the Wave!* (for junior highers to college-agers—also by Bethany House Publishers).

Snoozers Are Losers

There's one hitch in this plan to fathom your future.

Surrendering to God may seem like the right thing to do. Even back in Bible times, though, people thought *they didn't need to choose God's side anytime soon.* They weren't in any hurry to stop being God's foe and accept the friendship and forgiveness offered in Jesus.

Peter wrote that people would scoff at the promise of Christ's return. He assured his readers that judgment and joy were sure to come (2 Peter 3:3–9). He also pointed out this: Christ's "slowness" to show up is an opportunity for human beings to stop fighting against him. There's one huge reason for God's delay: "But do not forget this one thing, dear friends: With the Lord a day is like a thousand years, and a thousand years are like a day. The Lord is not slow in keeping his promise, as some understand slowness. He is patient with you, not wanting anyone to perish, but everyone to come to repentance" (2 Peter 3:8–9).

God has given time. God might continue to give time— that's his choice. The hitch is that you could feel you have all *zzzzz* time in *zzzzz* world.

If you snooze, you lose.

Clinging to an Ice Cube

Picture this: You're an explorer—an investigator of all things cool in Antarctica. One day the ice shelf where you've pitched camp crashes into the sea. The crack and boom of shearing ice sounded like someone ripping off your head, but you survive. You and a herd of penguins are marooned on Iceberg Island.

You aren't sure how long you can last. But the ice chunk is hundreds of yards across, and with all your supplies on board you figure you can bob on your Popsicle paradise forever.

Except for one thing.

Ice melts.

Floating solo on a berg is no funky dream. It's life. You probably won't ever wake up to penguins sharing your space. But your iceberg—your life—drifts each day further into the future. And know what? It's always shrinking. Every day there's a chance you'll slip into the sea. You'd be gone in an instant. You might float over an underwater volcano, a heat vent from the earth's innards. You'd disappear in a boil. Some days whole chunks break off, and like it or not, every day you melt more.

You might not live to see the Big End. But you and every other mortal will meet your own little end. You could slip in the shower and irreparably bonk your brain. Choke on a chicken bone. Die tonight in a car accident. Succumb to cancer, heart disease, or ten thousand other not-so-nice ways to die. Sure, you could live to a hundred and ten. The end will still come. And you can't fathom your end any more than you can remember the day you were born. Your life is melting away. You're clinging to an ice cube. One day your little boat won't float.

The end of the world is near. Your own end is probably nearer. Way nearer than you want to think (Luke 12:19–20).

One day
in some way
God will say,
"Time's up!"

Shredding Time

You've shot through the tube of time. Fastforwarded to your future. Flown to the edge of eternity.

You probably know that just about every science fiction show you could ever watch says it isn't wise to tamper with time. Time travelers who scamper forward or back are honor-bound to keep time's secrets. They aren't supposed to steal from the future—or intrude on the past. They'd alter the time-space continuum and unravel the thread of history.

Sci-fi fans say if you figure out the future you'll wreck it.

God has told you your future so you can alter it.

As far as he's concerned, it's more than fine to go ahead and shred time. To rearrange your future if you don't like what you see.

When you know you belong to God you can face without fear any future that time brings. And you'll be prepared for the ultimate *sprrroing* of time's clock. Jesus said this:

> "There will be signs in the sun, moon, and stars. On earth, nations will be afraid and confused because of the roar and fury of the sea. People will be so afraid they will faint, wondering what is happening to the world, because the powers of heaven will be shaken. Then people will see the Son of Man coming in a cloud with power and great glory.

When these things begin to happen, look up and hold your heads high, because the time when God will free you is near!"

Luke 21:25–28, NCV

If you live close to Jesus—trusting in his forgiveness, being scrubbed up inside and out to live a new life—you'll be confident and unashamed at his coming (1 John 2:28).

God rules.

Satan roasts.

Get ready.

Want to Read More?

Here are some sane, interesting books loaded with information about the end of everything:

Doomsday: The End of the World—A View Through Time (Servant Publications, 1993) is by Russell Chandler, an award-winning journalist and former religion writer for the *Los Angeles Times*. His book scopes out end-of-the-world hype through the long lens of history. Definitely the book to buy.

Ed Hinson's *Final Signs: Amazing Prophecies of the End Times* (Harvest House, 1996) does a great job separating biblical facts from assumptions and speculation.

William M. Alnor wrote *Soothsayers of the Second Advent* (Revell, 1989) to expose "doomsday dating, pin-the-tail-on-the-Antichrist, and other non-biblical games that Christians play." It's currently out of print, but checking the library at your church or a Christian college is worth the hunt.

If you want to dig deep into end times theology, chew on the chapters on eschatology and the kingdom of God in

George Eldon Ladd's *A Theology of the New Testament* (Eerdmans, 1974).

And if you want to impress your friends with fun factoids—like the ones back in chapter one—grab a copy of *What Counts: The Complete Harper's Index* (Henry Holt and Company, 1991).

Acknowledgments

Thanks to Rochelle Glöege, Barb Lilland, and Bethany House Publishers for bequeathing yet another opportunity to speak to youth, and to Janna Anderson, Cathy Engstrom, Christopher Soderstrom, and Natasha Sperling for snorting at my writing.

Thanks to Seth Barnes and all the staff at Adventures In Missions for some timely affirmation in ministry. I'll be back. Especially if we can go back to that little barbecue place.

Thanks to Tom Phillips, Dean Halverson, Tim Wildmon, and Hank Hanegraaff for quick but reassuring comments that I was on the right track. Maybe. Or maybe not. Well, probably.

Thanks to the late George Eldon Ladd and his work that lives on through the professors of Fuller Theological Seminary.

Thanks to Russell Chandler for writing sanely on many insane topics.

Thanks to the best wife and kids in the world. Lyn, thanks for living all of this weird life with me, and being patient as I plodded through wacko books and videos and banged my head for long hours to make this subject understandable. Thanks to my wonderful kiddies—Nate, Karin, and Elise—for all your hugs and helpfulness. *Mmmbop*.

And thanks to Jesus, who says, "Yes, I am coming soon" (Revelation 22:20).

Amen. Come, Lord Jesus.

Look forward and live holy,
Kevin Walter Johnson
October, 1997